The Adoption Experience

Families Who Give Children a Second Chance

Ann Morris

Jessica Kingsley Publishers
London and Philadelphia

Adoption UK
The Daily Telegraph

The right of Ann Morris to be identified as author of this work has been asserted by her in accordance with the Copyright, Designs and Patents Act 1988.

First published in the United Kingdom in 1999 by
Jessica Kingsley Publishers Ltd,
116 Pentonville Road, London
N1 9JB, England
and
325 Chestnut Street,
Philadelphia,
PA 19106, USA.

www.jkp.com

Library of Congress Cataloging in Publication Data
A CIP catalog record for this book is available from the Library of Congress

British Library Cataloguing in Publication Data
Morris, Ann
The adoption experience : families who give children a second chance
1. Adoption – Great Britain 2. Adoption – Law and legislation – Great Britain
I. Title 262.7'34'0941

ISBN 1 85302 783 9

Printed and Bound in Great Britain by
Athenaeum Press, Gateshead, Tyne and Wear

of related interest

First Steps in Parenting the Child Who Hurts: Tiddlers and Toddlers
Caroline Archer, Adoption UK
ISBN 1 85302 801 0

Next Steps in Parenting the Child Who Hurts: Tykes and Teens
Caroline Archer, Adoption UK
ISBN 1 85302 802 9

Violence in Children and Adolescents
Edited by Ved Varma
ISBN 1 85302 344 2 pb

Troubles of Children and Adolescents
Edited by Ved Varma
ISBN 1 85302 323 X pb

How We Feel: An Insight into the Emotional World of Teenagers
Edited by Jacki Gordon and Gillian Grant
ISBN 1 85302 439 2 pb

Child Adoption
A Guidebook for Adoptive Parents and Their Advisors
Rene A.C. Hoksbergen
ISBN 1 85302 415 5 pb

Parenting Teenagers
Bob Myers
ISBN 1 85302 366 3 pb

Raising Responsible Teenagers
Bob Myers
ISBN 1 85302 429 5 pb

The Adoption Experience

Contents

This book is dedicated to Hilary Chambers and Sheilagh Crawford, the founders of Adoption UK, who have helped change the face of adoption in Britain today.

Acknowledgements

First and foremost, thanks are due to all the families in Adoption UK who have shared their adoption experiences in this book and who make adoption work on a daily basis. Without them this book would not have been written.

I would also like to thank Richard White of White & Sherwin Solicitors, Croydon, who has kindly used his expertise as a lawyer with specialist knowledge of adoption to write for this book on adoption law (See Appendix 2). Many thanks too to the illustrators whose drawings we have used, including Joy Hasler, Anni Robinson, Jo Ings, Kathy Parker, Patricia Swanton, B Morall, Caroline Owen, Stephen Owen, Cadwgan Thomas, Vicky Waite and Owen Davies. Enormous thanks are due to Philly Morrall for her inspiration, support and occasional push to make this book happen, to all those in the Adoption UK offices in Lower Boddington and to those who edit the *Adoption UK Journal*. I am also deeply grateful to Hilary Chambers, who gave up a great amount of her time, trekking regularly across London to go through the detail of each chapter. She deserves a first-class degree in tact and diplomacy, and this book would never have happened without her.

On a more personal note, I would like to thank Susannah Charlton of Telegraph Books, who put her full weight behind the book, went in search of the right publisher and found it (and thanks to Jessica Kingsley for publishing the book). I would also like to thank Christine Fernandes, who has helped by typing in many of the stories and by proof-reading the book. Last, but always first to me, I would like to thank my husband Daniel and daughters Isobel and Laura, who have given me the valuable space and time to complete this book.

Introduction

Adoption touches almost everyone. Even if we are not involved in the triangle of adoption – adoptee, adopter, birth parent – ourselves, most of us have friends, family, neighbours or colleagues who are.

This book attempts to honestly set down through first-hand experiences what adoption is all about, primarily from the adopter's point of view. Adopters have written about the excitement of meeting a child for the first time, the joy of creating a new adoptive family, the trauma when things go wrong and the heartbreak they feel when they can't put things right.

Each story is edited from articles and letters written to Adoption UK over the past ten years and is told in the words of the writers. Adoption UK, formerly known as Parent to Parent Information on Adoption Services (PPIAS), was set up in 1971 by Hilary Chambers and Sheilagh Crawford. They both felt very strongly about the number of children in the care system who were not considered suitable for adoption – black children of all ages, older white children, sibling groups and children with disabilities. These two women and their families set out to raise awareness of the needs of these children. Attitudes have changed dramatically since those early days, and society now believes that all children have a right to family life and that no child should be considered 'unadoptable'. But hundreds of children still wait for adoption. The process is not easy or quick, and the primary aim of Adoption UK remains the finding of families for these children.

Adoption UK has also enabled families to form a network of support for one another. The experiences they have described in this book were originally written to share their joy with other adoptive families and help them to deal with the unusual challenges they face. Many of the challenges, misunderstandings and joys of adoption are common to all parents, but there is always an extra layer of concern for adopters. 'Tom is being impossible' is the sort of statement that any mother will make about her child from time to time, putting it down to overtiredness, a falling-out with friends, a bad experience at school or the catch-all of adolescence. Adoptive parents have a second type of question nagging at them: does this impossible behaviour have anything to do with his adoption or with a time before he was adopted; is it stress triggered by some distant emotional memory that he can't articulate and that we (the adoptive parents) know nothing about?

Together, we hope, these adoption stories not only give some personal insights into how adopters answer this challenge, feel and cope, but also show what a success story adoption of even the most difficult children can be – without hiding the facts that things don't always work out and that the stresses involved can break people apart.

Adoption is a roller-coaster experience – there are ups and downs, thrills and spills – but then so is life. Who has a family untouched by death, divorce, illness, irresponsibility and irrational behaviour? But equally, who has a life untouched by joy, love, friendship, laughter and delight?

This book is about the families in Adoption UK. The experiences often describe a moment in time, although some take a more long-term, reflective look at adoption. All names have been changed except where the writer has requested that their name be used and in Chapter 16, in which adoptees talk about their own experiences of adoption.

This collection of real-life stories was instigated by Philly Morrall and nurtured and fine-tuned by Adoption UK's founder, Hilary Chambers. It was inspired by *Adoption: The Inside Story*, an earlier collection of adopters' experiences published in 1985.

Adopting is not for everyone – but we hope that this book encourages those thinking about adoption to consider it more seriously and those who are adopting to stick with it.

CHAPTER 1

You Want to Adopt

There is a short moment of pure joy and excitement for most potential adopters when they first decide that they want to adopt a child. It's a moment as special as any in an adult's life, but as brief as a hot summer's day. The path forward is no yellow brick road to the land of Oz, but is as unpredictable and varied as the British weather – with a strong tendency towards thick fog and storms.

Getting 'taken on' by an adoption agency is the first of three hurdles that all adopters face – and for some this first hurdle can be mountain sized. Agencies differ in the sorts of families they prefer and in their methods of recruiting them. A potential adopter must be prepared to write dozens of letters stating their case in a bid to find an agency – a process which seems bizarre when you consider that there are hundreds of children waiting for families. It sometimes seems that although most adoptees come from 'unusual', less than perfect families, adopters must be perfect and conform to the social mores of the Victorians.

'I'm fed up, cheesed off and ever so slightly depressed,' wrote one prospective adopter in a recent mock letter to members of an adoption panel. 'I have opted for a life choice that you seem to consider completely beyond the pale, something no other mother in the country has ever considered – work outside the home.'

But Adoption UK has also seen successful adoptions by the most unconventional people, whose chances look as impossible on paper as those of the proverbial camel passing through the eye of a needle: single adopters, disabled adopters, gay adopters and those whose own life stories make their friends reel with horror.

Perseverance and conviction that adoption is right for you and your family is the best weapon in this strange and very personal battle.

Once taken on, the second hurdle is the assessment process, in which the potential adopter faces in-depth appraisal and preparation. Completion of the central part, the standard Form F, involves a large amount of self-analysis. It can be an educative and illuminating experience, helping potential adopters to discover and understand the special parenting skills they have and will need to offer to a child placed for adoption. But for some the experience of assessment can be nerve-racking and intrusive. The fruitfulness of this essential preliminary to adoption is often dependent on the relationship between the potential adopter and the social worker carrying out the task.

This preparation concludes on the day the panel meets to decide whether or not to recommend your approval.

That hurdle jumped, there is a third hurdle waiting – finding the child. There is no limit on how long you have to wait between being approved as a potential adopter and being linked with children looking for adoption. For many, this is the most frustrating and often upsetting time. Children gaze out longingly from *Be My Parent,* a bimonthly photolisting of children needing new families, and the *Adoption UK Journal,* but calls and letters are fruitless. The worst moment is when you are told, often with little compassion, that your face doesn't fit and that for one reason or another you are not quite what they had in mind for the child or children. Many agencies will interview two or more sets of families for a child and then choose 'the best'. Losing can be a devastating blow to your personal self-esteem. 'You begin to hold back. You don't jump around with joy every time a social worker calls to discuss a child,' said one adoptive mother who wrote over 100 letters before her adoptive children 'found' her.

Finally, you enter the life game of adoptive parenthood. It's not easy, but for the great majority of parents it is immensely rewarding. Some go back to adopt again and again and again.

Each person's experience of finding an agency, getting through the system and reaching the child at the centre of the maze differs enormously. In this chapter we look at a few.

● ● ●

An everyday story of would-be adopters

This is the everyday story of two would-be adoptive parents and three children looking for an adoptive family.

My husband and I approached our local social services about adoption. One introductory meeting, four evening preparation sessions and some home study later – a mere six months – we were approved as adoptive parents for one or two children aged five or under. However, months passed and there seemed no immediate prospect of a placement. We were living in limbo, waiting for something to happen.

In the very first *Adoption UK Journal* that we received we saw 'our' three children. We felt that we were made for each other. We just knew that we could love these children and help them with the problems they had.

When we first contacted the children's family placement worker we were told that there were already some strong candidates, but they took our details anyway and said they'd probably come down for a brief visit. Not much hope here, we thought sadly, and resigned ourselves to more living in limbo.

They did come, but made lots of clucking noises about us only having been approved for two children (do many people set out with the idea of getting approval to take large sibling groups?), living in a rural area (even though we live in a large, lively village) and not having much experience of children. We had in fact regularly looked after a slightly older fostered boy for weekends and weeks at a time, and anyway, are there so many people who've brought up lots of children who want to take on three more? Last but by no means least, the social worker told us how the other strong candidates had lots of life insurance.

When the social worker left we wondered why on earth they had come! However, they came back several times, still clucking but obviously considering us. The suspense was unbearable.

Four months later the social worker decided to go with us subject to our being approved by their panel twice, once to extend our approval from two to three children, and then again to agree the actual placement of our three children with us. More nail-biting suspense.

A word of advice to prospective adopters: stay at work as long as possible or take up a time-consuming hobby. Both fill the seemingly endless waiting time and provide a necessary distraction from 'will they, won't they, why, when' and all the other questions, which absorb every waking moment until you have become an anxious obsessive, unable to conduct normal human relationships.

It's traumatic to have your whole future hanging in the balance. You feel totally powerless because you're completely in someone else's hands.

The suspense did finally come to an end and they did approve us, meaning that the placement would go ahead. After months of waiting everything went swiftly, as if we were living in video fast-forward mode. And of course, the anxiety of 'will they or won't they approve us?' was replaced by 'what if the children don't like us?' A truly terrifying thought.

A three and a half years circle

Summer 1991. The little girl was the ninth mixed-race child we had phoned up about in our search for the last member of our family. But in spite of our semi-Asian lifestyle, the product of many years abroad and three mixed-race adopted children (we also have two natural ones), middle-aged white parents were, of course, not considered first choice. Anyway, a matching family had already been found.

Summer 1992. After several more phone calls with similar results we enquired about an English girl, only to find that 80 other people had had the same idea. To our amazement, we also found out that having been approved by our local social services for a mixed-race child, we could not switch to a white one anyway without going back to panel. It was then that Adoption UK told us to 'hang on, stick to what you feel you have to offer and don't let anyone tell you otherwise'. We did – for three and a half years and 29 attempts!

Summer 1993. A tiny article in a tiny biannual magazine, a false name without a face – how easily we could have missed child number 29. A few discussions with social workers followed, but because of an impossible legal situation we were not even shown her picture so as not to raise our hopes in vain.

Summer 1994. In May, the legal situation resolved, we finally saw some photographs and recognised her as child number nine of three years ago. In June we were passed by the panel.

The selection lottery

Having been approved as potential adopters nine months ago my husband and I are still waiting for children. We have so far been considered for three sets of brothers and sisters.

Most recently we were given details of two children we dearly wanted to adopt. After considerable delay two social workers arrived at our home. We shared with them more information about ourselves and allowed them to look around the house. It was only at this stage that we were told that they were also considering another couple. Three days later, after a painful weekend, we were told that the other couple had 'won'.

I know that in defence of this practice social workers would state that their main responsibility is to the children involved. However, to me it does not seem incompatible with this duty to consider also the ordeal to which the prospective adopters are being subjected. Presumably, in expressing a wish to adopt the children we are expected, despite not having met them, to develop the beginnings of some kind of bond, as would any parent towards an expected child. In treating us in this way social workers are subjecting us to sequential bereavement which at times seems unbearable. Adoptive parents usually know about loss. I have lost five pregnancies, as well as two other prospective adoptive children through a similar process; it seems against the spirit of social work to inflict this upon people repeatedly.

These children's futures may have been secured and the social workers may feel satisfied that they have achieved their objectives. However, they have done the wider cause of adoption no good at all, as despite being approved, I personally will not be able to stand much more and may withdraw from the whole process.

Never give up

John was placed with us when he was 15 months old and we adopted him at 26 months. Nothing very remarkable perhaps, except that we have a mentally and physically handicapped daughter, Emma, who was then 12 years old, we ourselves were aged 39 and 41, and my husband is diabetic.

We had been approved 18 months earlier as an adoptive family by a county council for whom we had fostered a total of 17 children over seven years. It was at this point that we seemed to hit a brick wall. Remarks made by a child psychologist, whilst we were fostering, about the effect that a handicapped child would have on the life of a normal child, were brought up repeatedly, even though our GP and health visitor both wrote to the adoption agency in support of our application. In May 1988 we wrote to 35 different agencies saying that we had been approved as adoptive parents.

Eventually, following a chance phone call to an adoption department, we were contacted regarding John. This was followed by a nerve-racking few days before we heard that they had approved our Form F. The case went to the panel in January 1989. We met John four days later and brought him home five days after that first meeting.

Success at last! It was worth the fight and all the hassle.

We now have a super family: the children get on with each other and we are always being told how like us John is. I'm sure the moral of this is 'never give up'.

Pre-adoption courses

We have a son of our own and have looked after many children as childminders, and therefore found it difficult to understand why we should need a pre-adoption course. There were so many children needing homes – why couldn't we have one and just get on with being good parents?

But what an education the course turned out to be. We and four other couples met over a two-month period, exploring our past histories, making family trees and considering how a child coming into our families would fit in. It emerged that it would not just be us as parents who adopted, but our entire family. Who would have problems accepting a child who was not blood related? Who would support and who would oppose our decision? This led to much discussion amongst our own family and friends as we tried to explore what adoption would mean to them.

We were privileged to hear the experiences of adopted people, adoptive parents and birth mothers who had given up their babies for adoption – brave people who were open and honest with us, showing the many kinds of pain and pleasure adoption can bring. We came to realise that an adopted child has a past, with all its memories and relationships, and that this cannot and indeed should not be forgotten: their family tree must one day be traced. This led to many heated discussions on 'open adoption' involving many different points of view.

We also covered the subject of child abuse in all its various forms and the behavioural effects this may have on children. We were given an insight into how we would cope with a damaged child. Between the meetings we talked together about how we felt as a couple, putting our lives into perspective and deciding whether we really wanted to carry on with adoption.

All of this culminated in presenting ourselves to the group and the project team, who asked questions about our motives and belief in our ability to cope with adoption. Although this was nerve-racking, it was important to know whether everyone else saw us as we saw ourselves.

Next came the task of completing our application form, spending countless hours thinking about, writing and rewriting what we hoped would be a fair view of our lives and capabilities. The commitment required to complete this task was a good test of our determination, and the closeness we felt in sharing this effort was very rewarding. The sense of achievement we gained from finishing Form F overwhelmed us. With the full support of the team and group we went to the panel and are ecstatic to say we are now approved.

Coming to terms

I'm angry! Yet again I've been questioned on 'coming to terms with my infertility'. What is 'coming to terms' anyway? Can anyone define it for me? I'm infertile, and we've decided to make our family by adopting older children. Is the fact that we are different from some infertile couples so hard to understand? And why, just because we have reacted in the way we have, must we be wrong?

Would it have satisfied social workers if I'd grieved and wanted only to adopt a baby? I doubt it. Surely too much introspective talk is unproductive. What is important is how I am now: a very happy mother to an eleven-year-old, wanting to add another child to our family. I'm at ease with my infertility, so why does it concern the professionals so much? Could it be that finding people who have faced a problem and moved on from it highlights their own inadequacies? Or is it that they are blindly following a set of questions given to them? My anger abates when I remember that 'coming to terms with infertility' is their problem – it certainly isn't mine.

Panel talk

When I was first asked to join an adoption panel I felt both excited and honoured. It was only as my first panel meeting approached that I started to have second thoughts. What had I to bring to a panel of professionals?

There are nine other members of the panel: a medical adviser; a legal adviser; two clergymen, one of whom is our spiritual adviser, the other a member of the voluntary adoption agency's council; a senior social worker; our Assistant Regional Director; a project leader; a child placement consultant; and one other lay member who is also a teacher and foster carer. As for me, my role on the panel is that of a 'consumer'. I have an adopted son who has severe learning difficulties and epilepsy.

Being a parent equips you with all kinds of skills and insights that you either take for granted or don't realise that you have. I knew what the parents were talking about: I had been there. However, I do have to be careful to be objective. I have to remember that our coping mechanisms and abilities vary. For instance, the things that get me down may not necessarily affect others in the same way.

Our panel meets once a month. We receive continuous updates from a social worker from a family's initial application, so any complications are resolved long before the application comes to panel. At our meetings, we match a family with a child, or children in the case of siblings. Panel members study the papers prior to the meeting. Following the presentation and clarification of issues by the case social worker, there are questions and then an open discussion. The panel has to make a unanimous decision on the strength of the facts and opinions presented. We always have an update from social workers on children looking for families and hear how prospective adopters and parents with whom children have been placed are progressing.

Any recommendations that we make are later ratified by our Director, and the families concerned usually know the outcome within a few days. Ultimately, no matter who we are or what we do, each member of the panel strives to reach the decision that will give the child the best future.

The positives of adoption

Like many couples, we assumed that we would have children until we had to face the challenge of infertility. Eventually we reached a point at which we decided to stop treatment, thus ending the emotional roundabout, and began to investigate adoption. My partner is adopted and so adoption was something that we already had some experience of.

After all the procedures, which took over three years, we were finally matched with a three-year-old girl, and since that day we have not looked back. She was well prepared and had been living in a good foster home for over a year. We recognise that we have been extremely lucky with the arrival of our daughter – she has enriched our lives tremendously. These are the positives of adoption as we see them:

- Adoption offers children who have experienced damaging events a safe, loving environment within which to explore and grow.

- Adoption offers a way out for those birth parents who have been through the agonising process of having their children removed, and who may be painfully aware of the fact that they cannot look after their children themselves.

- Physically, the female carer is spared the post-natal hormonal changes; she is alert and ready, with the stamina to cope with the demands of caring for a young child.

- With adoption there is no genetic 'baggage' to constrain a child's development; phrases such as 'he is just like his father' are not valid. They are free to be what they can with your help.

- Adoptive parents are very much aware that they have received a most precious gift and in some ways this makes us more appreciative of our children. This can be particularly so if there has been a long haul through infertility.

- Adoption requires careful matching by social workers so that there is a good chance of the placement being successful.

- For those adoptive parents who have experienced infertility there is a chance to make up for what seem like wasted years and be like their friends again, enjoying the real benefits of family life in a parental rather than an avuncular role.

- The very long pre-adoption process gives you the space and time to discuss issues such as contact and child-rearing practices, make plans for dealing with challenging behaviour, plan for a consistent approach, and so on.

That's it for now; there are probably more positives that in time I will come to discover. Right now I am enjoying our daughter's company.

Is everyone adopted?

Lying in bed one night, unable to sleep, I started thinking about the many ways in which adoption has touched our lives, and, in particular, about the sheer numbers of people we know who are part of one or another adoption triangle. I was amazed, and wonder whether our family is unusual in being so densely surrounded by adoption. Is this simply chance, or do we somehow exercise a magnetic attraction because of our own involvement? If enough adoptive families are concentrated in a small area, does adoption 'go critical' and start a chain reaction? Will we begin adopting each other, or start forcibly adopting innocent bystanders? I wonder how many families can match this for numbers:

1. Our own birth families. One of my wife's cousins has adopted, as have two of my cousins on different sides of the family. One of my nephews is currently in the process of adopting not only his two stepchildren but also another sibling pair. Another nephew with one child and six stepchildren is also fostering a sibling pair.

2. Our childhoods. Of my wife's best friends in school, one was an adoptee and another the child of an adoptee. I knew a girl who was a birth mother. I was good friends during an adolescent summer school with a boy who was the adopted son of parents who were both adoptees themselves. One of my dormitory mates at university was an adoptee, and so was another boy in the church boys' choir in which I sang.

3. Our current neighbourhood. Within a hundred yards of us live or have until very recently lived another seven families affected by adoption. Next door was a university professor adoptee (he now lives about half a mile away); next door but one on the other side lives a family with five born-to and two adopted children; another five houses down the street lives an elderly birth mother; across the street a family has just moved in with one born-to and three adopted children; and a couple of houses down from them is a family in which the father is an adoptee. The manager of our local leisure centre is an adoptive father. A widower in our village is an adoptive grandfather: his son and daughter-in-law adopted two brothers while we were living three doors down from him.

4. Chapel. There are at least three other adoptive families in our chapel, all of whose children attend the same school as our own. Our circuit of visiting preachers includes two adoptive fathers.

5. The town. In addition to the above families, within a one-mile radius we know an elderly adoptee friend of my mother, a single parent with two adult transracially adopted children, an adult transracial adoptee,

another transracial adoptive family and a family with two adoptive sons, one of whom climbs mountains in the Himalayas. The wife of our church organist, a lady we have known for over 20 years and who is now my mother's primary carer in her residential home, recently revealed to my mother that she is an adoptee; she has been contacted by birth relatives and has just begun to meet some of them. In our first home as a married couple our next-door neighbour was a former foster child, who followed keenly our early (fruitless) attempts at adoption. The village in which we lived also included a vicar with three adopted children.

6. At work. At my wife's secondary school there is another adoptive-parent teacher and at least two other families with adopted children. At my university there are at least three adoptive-parent lecturers, including one in my own department. And among the non-teaching staff there is at least one other adoptive father.

That makes, I think, over 30 separate families, allowing for overlap, all related to us or living or working within a mile of us. And those are just the ones we know personally. Also excluded are dozens of other adoptive families from further afield who we have got to know through Adoption UK. No wonder one of our own four children once asked me: 'Daddy, are *all* children adopted?'

CHAPTER 2

First Meetings, First Months, Falling in Love

It can be as easy as one, two, three or as hard as taking a degree in maths for the innumerate. Whether through birth or adoption, coming face to face for the first time with a child who will be an intrinsic part of the rest of your life is one of the most memorable experiences any adult can have.

It's more exciting and tense than watching your country play football in a World Cup Final and as emotional a landmark as the day you fall in love for the first time.

Dreams of what it will be like disappear as reality takes over. Nothing can totally prepare you for that first meeting.

'It's an impossible task, this painting a portrait of another human being. It's like an arranged marriage: the parents tell their son that the girl is tall, with dark brown hair and a full figure. She likes Mozart and her eggs well boiled and is a dab hand with a needle. "Yes", thinks the bewildered youth, "but what is she like?" It's the same with a child. No one can ever tell you what it will be like to meet and still less to live with him or her.' So writes one seasoned adopter.

It is at this 'arranged marriage' stage that a good social worker, with an innate understanding of what makes people tick, can make all the difference. She or he has to separate and deal with real fears and first-meeting nerves. However well arranged the adoption, niggling at most prospective adopters' consciences is the underlying anxiety that they might not be able to love and bond with a child not born to them.

Once the child has moved in and the 'marriage' has taken place, the reality of living together begins. These can be joyous times but they can also be testing. Society tends to expect far more parental tolerance and understanding from adopters than it does from natural parents.

As one mother of seven (four by birth, one adopted and two in the process of being adopted) wrote: 'Growing to love your little cuckoo is not easy and rarely happens overnight. With adoptive children, just as with birth children, each process is different. It can be very hard to admit that you are not bonding with this child you have fought so long to get. But if you scratch the surface of any doting parent you will uncover anxious days of doubt. Bonding takes time. Parents as well as children need to go through stages of attachment.'

In this chapter adoptive parents recount some magical and not so magical meetings and first months.

● ● ●

I don't like salad

The big day arrived at last. The day before, I was a career girl. I was about to become the adoptive mother of two children aged seven and four years.

I had been asked to meet the social worker at 10 a.m. at the foster parents' home, where the children would be waiting. Driving there, my heart was in my mouth. What were these two children really like? All I had was a tiny photograph and a descriptive paragraph. Would I like them? Would they like me and their adoptive dad? What if I didn't like them? What if they didn't like us? Were we ready for all this?

In answer to the last question, yes, we were! Or at least we thought we were. We were over-ready if anything. Their bedrooms were ready, with a new teddy on each pillow waiting to be cuddled. The freezer was full of fish fingers and ice cream. There were cards and piles of presents from relatives anxious to meet them. There was a file full to the brim with training notes from social services and a hotline phone number for the social workers. We were ready – well, as ready as we could ever be.

When we arrived at the home of the foster parents, a scruffy-faced little boy was standing at the lounge window. His foster mum said he had been standing there all morning. 'It's a big day for him,' she added. It was a big day for us too. My knees felt as if they did not belong to me. The boy bounded around his foster home slamming doors, knocking things over, and talking incessantly about anything and everything as we sat down for a cup of tea. He wouldn't look at us or talk to us directly, whereas his sister covered us with her cuddly toys, sat on our laps and asked us if we were really her new forever mum and dad.

We had a long walk across the beach, hand in hand with the little girl. The boy kept his distance. He was really loud and naughty and had to be reprimanded by his foster mother on several occasions, which resulted in a long silent sulk that lasted all the way back to the house.

By this time I felt as if I'd run an emotional London Marathon. Would he be okay? Would I be okay with him? I hadn't expected a wonderful mother/son relationship immediately – this would take time – but nevertheless I felt very uneasy.

As we prepared to say goodbye, promising to return the next evening for bath time, the little girl burst into tears and clung to us; the boy was withdrawn and asked if he could now watch the television.

I wound down the window of the car to wave goodbye when the boy approached the car. 'I don't like salad,' he said positively. We smiled. It was going to be okay.

And four years later, yes, it is.

Update 1999: It is hard to believe that this little boy is now a hotel manager who still occasionally needs his mum (or her cheque book!).

We wouldn't change a thing

After trying unsuccessfully to have children for five years we decided to try adoption. Failing to have children did not upset us especially, and adoption was certainly not a second best. We felt ready to take on the responsibility of a family – adoptive or natural, family was the key issue.

We applied to our local authority when we were both 35. Very early on, we had decided we would like to adopt two siblings. We were finally approved as adopters six months later.

Four months after that another local authority contacted our social worker about placing with us Mark, who was nearly three, and Debbie, who was a year younger. The meeting we had with our own social worker and two workers from the other authority was very difficult because we were so excited and bemused by things. Our social worker was superb, asking all the questions about the children that we were too excited and naive to think of.

We first met Mark and Debbie just before Christmas. The foster parents and their children greeted us as nervously as we greeted them, and Mark and Debbie soon gathered that something was up. However, they quickly warmed to us – we'd taken colouring pens and books, and tying their shoelaces helped! The meeting was a real strain but we felt instinctively that we were right for each other. Both social workers agreed with our instincts but insisted that we take a week or so to think it over.

After the Christmas break, during which we had thought of little other than the children, we made plans with their foster parents for a series of meetings in which we could get to know each other. At first we visited Mark and Debbie for half-days, during which we began taking them to the toilet, the shops and the park, reading to them, playing with them and just being around. Next, they visited us with their foster family for Sunday lunch, and then stayed with us for two separate days. After two weeks we tried a weekend with an overnight stay, which went well, and the next Thursday evening they arrived for two nights – and for good if things seemed to be going well enough.

They have stayed with us ever since. Parting with the foster parents for what turned out to be the last time was difficult; they were understandably upset, but we were lucky to have a kind, sensitive and very supportive foster family to deal with.

The series of meetings was physically, mentally and emotionally wearing, but the social workers were smashing and the foster family did everything they could to help. Indeed, they were such a good foster family that we felt a little intimidated as we were so inexperienced.

Mark and Debbie now seem happy and relaxed, although there are still some times of real stress. For instance, when one of us was ill Mark became very difficult in general – everything became a potential confrontation and it was wearing as well as worrying. Social workers, family and friends all said that this was to be expected. We blundered on, giving lots of hugs and kisses in between sorting out Mark's problems and taking every day as it came.

Friends have helped by having us to tea and encouraging their children to play with Mark and Debbie, only one person being a bit wary of the children and overprotective of her daughter. Family members have become firm favourites by showing obvious affection for the children – which has quickly turned into genuine love.

Our thoughts on the first twelve months are as follows. Much to our own surprise we are a happy, noisy, sometimes argumentative and quarrelsome family. Everyone tells us that we're normal. Life has changed totally. We share our feelings and are closer because of the children, but it has been difficult at times just coming to terms with the fact that all our time is family time. However, we're sure the fun and love will continue, as well as the problems. Apart from the chance to have the occasional Sunday morning lie-in, we wouldn't change a thing.

Hard graft – but worth it

Our three children, siblings aged five, four and two, have been with us for six months. We have had some lovely times and also some horrendous ones!

The children had been removed from their birth mother 18 months before and had then been cared for by members of their extended first family rather than professional foster carers; so the introductory period was incredibly hard for everyone involved. After the first day's visit to the girls' home, on which we were accompanied by the social worker, we were left to go to the home by ourselves to play with them, take them out, and so on, all under the eyes of their first family. They found it increasingly difficult to help us and the children to get to know each other in any very positive way. Luckily, the local authority managed to give us the run of a family centre at weekends so we could be alone with the children. It also proved impossible for the first family to let us participate in the girls' routine. We weren't allowed to go to the home of our youngest child, so she came to us (at two years old) having never been put to bed, dressed, bathed or woken up by me at all – not an ideal situation.

The children were placed with us permanently four and a half weeks after the first meeting. I can honestly say that those weeks were probably one of the most stressful periods we've ever experienced. We had driven hundreds of miles, closed down my business, prepared our home for their arrival (installing stair gates, bunk beds, and so on) and had to cope with the deeply damaged first family. It was not the joyful, relaxed, special 'getting to know you' time we had so hoped for. Already slim, I lost 10lb in weight.

It was only after placement that further detailed files on the children's lifestyle prior to coming into care were given to us. And it was only then that it was finally disclosed (after a lot of questioning) that the children's extended family, including the children's carers, had been sexually abused when they were children.

We did initially have a lot of challenging times with our two eldest. Even now, we find some things they do hard to accept. However, we have settled down together very well; the children have all blossomed and grown alarmingly! As they were adopted straight from the family, a lot of work on their lives had not been done, and although it was hard we are glad that we were the ones to help our children make sense of it all.

Certainly, the fact that there are three of them, while hard graft for us, has meant that they can support each other. Their new life is not as strange and threatening as it would have been for a lone child. The advantage for us is that they are rarely all horrid at once – there is always one 'little darling' to remind you why you did it and give you the strength to go on. And there have been times when we have not been able to believe how well things have gone and how complete a family we are now.

The day the co-ordinator cried

'Would you talk to a couple,' the social worker asked, 'who are approved for adoption and are seeking a child under five years old?'

Mr and Mrs P arrived at my home. Once my children had inspected them in their usual fashion (i.e. in and out of the house for drinks, lollies and the loo) we were left in peace to talk.

Mr P was deaf, and Mrs P's hearing impaired. Mrs P signed for her husband, but he was a great lip-reader. They were seeking a deaf child or a child of impaired hearing. I gave them as much information as I could and they left. Later, I had a phone call from Mrs P, telling me that they were being seen with regard to a four-year-old boy.

In the last week of the summer holidays, my doorbell rang and there on the doorstep was a little boy. I could hardly see his face behind the huge pot plant he was holding. Behind him were Mr and Mrs P; they had travelled over to introduce their new son and say thank you.

Quite a bit of cuddling and sniffing went on. I was delighted for them, and shed some happy tears when they departed.

The right equation

Before we met our adopted daughter we had been told that she was prone to extremely violent tantrums, was very delayed with speech and completely refused to potty-train. She was two and a half years old. We were also told that she had only recently bonded with her foster mother of 20 months, and that she was slow to take to people and would probably not even look at us for the first few visits. In reality, she sat on our knees at the first visit and took to us straight away, with no reservations. When our own two children met Lucy a few days later it was love at first sight. We have had virtually no jealousy at all – the children are already asking if we can adopt again!

Now, six months after placement, we feel that we have had a fairly easy ride in view of the problems we were told about. While we were waiting to meet Lucy and pondering these problems, a friend (also an adopter) told me to meet her with an open mind, for once a child feels secure, problems often resolve themselves. Lucy was completely out of nappies after ten weeks for daytime and five months for nights, her speech was considered normal 12 weeks after placement, the tantrums ceased after eight weeks (control of temper took about five months) and she bonded with us incredibly quickly.

We also feel very lucky that we all have just the right 'chemistry' together.

Days of doubt

On reading articles and books on bonding and attachment, I have often been left with the impression that whilst the child is understandably having problems bonding with a new family, the parents remain firmly and unwaveringly in love with their child.

Am I really alone in being the only 'awful' parent out there who ends some days positively disliking one or more of the children? Am I really the only parent to be irritated to the point of screaming by my children's endless, repetitious and pointless attention-seeking chatter? Am I alone in indulging myself with the odd evening discussion on slow and horrendous tortures for 'the next time he does that'? Does no other adoptive parent ever wonder why on earth they ever started on this particular rocky path?

Post-adoption depression

Post-adoption depression. You've never heard of it? Neither had I. Perhaps if I had I would have recognised the symptoms and been able to ask for help sooner.

Infertility – tests, hopes, dreams, waiting. Finally, the decision to adopt – positive action! Unfortunately, it took our agency three years to complete our assessment; by the time we were approved we were weary of the whole system and thought these mythical children would never be a reality.

Our papers were requested for consideration for two children, a girl and a boy. Uncertainty about the boy's future delayed progress for six months. Finally, we were matched with them. The little girl was three and the boy 20 months. Unless you have been there it's impossible to understand such total destruction of life as you know it. Suddenly, there are two dynamos in your previously peaceful and ordered life. Two children with very different needs – and somewhere along the line your own needs go unnoticed.

I'd prepared myself for being physically exhausted but never imagined the toll it would take on my mental health. I had no outlet for my feelings. Everyone I saw expected me to be so happy – I'd got what I wanted hadn't I? No! What I'd got were two strangers who called me 'Mummy' and said 'I love you' from the first day, who ruled my every second, day and night. The boy was impossible all the time, screaming, headbanging and refusing to eat. I couldn't keep up with the washing and cleaning.

Trying to find time for my husband or myself was impossible. This was very hard for us to accept as we had been a happy couple for over 12 years, and I began to resent the children for causing upset and arguments. Where were the good times, the loving family atmosphere, the family outings and celebrations? All I had was guilt. Why didn't I love these children? What had I done to my marriage and my life? I began to think the unthinkable – I wanted these children (and therefore all the problems) to go away. I lost nearly two stone in weight.

It all came to a head one Monday. The little boy was very unhappy, screaming and headbanging. Nothing I did was right and I just sat down with him and cried. I admitted defeat. I phoned the social worker and said that I couldn't carry on any longer.

A family had been our dream for so long – it had been mine since I was a little girl. This was the end of the road for my life, or so it seemed.

The social workers said that they would set up a support package. Then I had a call from a lady who I'd been to Adoption UK meetings with, who put me in touch with another member who had suffered from depression after a baby placement.

She told me her story. I couldn't believe it – she had felt the same way as me. I wasn't wicked or abnormal, I was suffering from depression.

My male GP's response was somewhat predictable: 'Post-natal depression? Absolute rubbish.' However, he finally agreed to put me on antidepressants while I sought help.

Social services agreed to leave the children with us for a while to see if things worked out. They arranged for the children to go to a nursery a couple of times a week so as to give me a break, and got us a place on a child and family therapy group. All these things helped to save our family. But above all, what saved us was the recognition that I was ill and that this was why I couldn't cope and saw everything so negatively. This was not the way I expected adoption to be through all those years of waiting. If only someone had warned me that I might feel these resentments and that I might not fall in love with the children overnight.

Thanks to my Adoption UK friends, our story has a happy ending. I gradually recovered, came off the tablets, and began to enjoy those special moments with my children and feel proud of our achievements. Two years on, we are a family. Our little girl has started school and our boy is at 'big boys' nursery.

Lost and found

The phone call came out of the blue. 'I've got a little girl on file who might suit you. She's just five, the daughter of a traveller. She's been in care since summer and a care order has been obtained.'

The dreary November day lit up for me. We had been waiting to foster a little girl for two years and were beginning to think there would never be a suitable child.

'Can you describe her?' I asked, hope rising in me.

'Well, she's lively and healthy, an only child and needs long-term care, possibly leading to adoption. She's doing well at school and has a strong link with her mother, whom she sees regularly.'

My mind began forming mental images. What was she like? Was she small, fat, thin, dark, fair? Was she affectionate? Withdrawn? Sad-looking? I learnt that she was small for her age, fairish, with large brown eyes.

We were told that we would hear nothing more until after Christmas. Then the first and telling meeting with the child was arranged.

I was unprepared for the kaleidoscope of feelings that this visit brought up in me, now that the reality was staring us in the face. Panic! How was my life going to be changed? How would it affect my three-year-old son? Would it be detrimental for him? Would it be better for him to stay an only child?

I had just returned from a writing weekend. It was my first weekend away from my son, and I was inspired by the freedom and joy of being creative again. Perhaps now I would have no time for myself ever again. No time for my own projects.

We drove, full of trepidation, to the meeting. We were pretending to be going for tea with her short-term foster carer. The little girl was sitting on the sofa. I remember her red-and-black spotted sweatshirt and the baggy dungarees hiding her shape. Her mouth was set in a thin, hard line. Her hair was a dull, lifeless mass. She was silent with tension and I thought, 'Help, she looks so tough!'

My husband knelt on the floor beside her and talked her into doing some sticky pictures with him. My son, conscious of all the tension and aware that it was going to affect him in some way, clung to me tightly, demanding my attention. I observed her from afar, watching her relax a little as she made pictures for us. I was still feeling tightly reserved and protective of my son.

It was only on parting that the change came about. As she stood on the doorstep her little face puckered into such sadness. She looked like a little waif. All the tightness and hardness around her mouth dissolved and she looked as though, inside, she was a small, sad and vulnerable child. She was revealing this to my husband, to whom she had warmed through play. My heart melted. I wanted to sweep her up into my arms there and then and take her home. That was the moment I became committed to bringing her into our lives.

The rocky path

When we married we planned to start a family almost straight away. After we had been married for three years I persuaded my husband that it was time to start on the adoption trail. Two years later we were finally approved to adopt up to three children between infancy and six years of age.

A month after this our social worker phoned. She started talking about two little boys aged two and a half and three and a half, and as she spoke my tears began to flow. Our little boys, our sons – we had found them!

And so it began, this love affair with two little boys. I didn't know more than a handful of facts about them, but it didn't matter. They felt right somehow, as if they were meant for us and we for them.

I love these children to the core of my being. Our worst day on record doesn't compare to not having them. However, there are times when I feel intensely angry with them and even dislike them. They can bring out the worst in me. Often, days are sprinkled with minor skirmishes; sometimes the skirmishes grow until a blanket of negative feelings shrouds the whole day. A description of my two lowest points will give some idea of what I mean!

The first was when Andrew bit Peter and in desperation I bit Andrew in return – much harder than I'd intended. It bruised his arm for several days and clouded the whole of our first summer together. I had only to wonder what our social worker would do if she saw Andrew's arm, or if he told her, for it all to dissolve into tears. I felt like a child abuser, and yet I also felt angry that anyone might even think of taking such a dearly-loved child away from me, and that I was in this position of dreading a visit from social services. I came from a background in which no one I knew would ever have dreamt of the possibility of social workers coming between them and their child.

The second 'low' was even lower than the first – it has the power to hurt me still, and probably always will. It happened three years after the boys arrived. Peter was six and a half. Of the two Peter has been the harder to bond with. This doesn't mean that I have any less commitment to him. In a sense it means that I have more – or at least that I make more of a conscious effort. I am often hard on Peter and have many regrets over times in which I've put him down or been unkind. We had spent a few days visiting my parents and my sister. Afterwards, I received a letter from my sister which threw me completely. She said she felt I had been very mean to Peter and should seek help to improve my relationship with him.

Three years after Peter's arrival, here was my sister (my closest confidant) saying that I should try to love him more. Had she any inkling of what I had been through, she could not have asked that of me. Three years of daily renewing a commitment to love, whatever the cost: I couldn't love more than that. In practice, I admit that it was also three years of daily failure, with much need for forgiveness on both sides!

I think the major reason why these two incidents took on such significance for me is that they challenged my belief in myself as a parent.

I cannot end, however, without adding something just as important – more so, in fact. I have not mentioned the fun times, the tender moments, the giggles, the joy and the pride I take in my two precious sons, who may cause me grief and anxiety but are nevertheless life, laughter and deepest fulfilment for me.

But adoption is different!

Whatever is known about the history of an adopted child, one certainty is that not everything will ever be known or understood. One real difficulty with the 'added layer' of adoption is the constant struggle to determine whether your child's behaviour is attributable to their past experiences, their moves in care or just a normal stage in their development.

We have struggled over the past five years, against great resistance, to get meaningful people in our children's lives to understand the implications of dealing with an adopted child. All too often, when adoptive families have difficulties, the external focus is on the family itself rather than on trying to understand these implications, the pressures with which adoptive parents struggle and the problems a damaged child can bring into a new unit for both themselves and the other members of that unit.

Without at least nine months' preparation, it is a struggle to adjust to suddenly having a child to care for and love. Maybe for some the bonding of love is instantaneous, but for us love came gradually and deepened as we got to know our children. The joy and support of our family and friends was much needed, but what we were not prepared for was how, almost imperceptibly, the fact of our children's adoption began to be ignored. It was not that we wanted to raise it and shout it from the rooftops at every opportunity, but their development, needs and feelings (not, of course, forgetting ours) were so rooted in their history that ignoring their adoption was not only impossible but also devalued their important life experiences.

Because our children were just under a year old when placed, the professionals largely took the view that their experiences prior to placement were of limited import. As adoptive parents we suffered from the apparently quite usual adopters' syndrome of feeling that we had to be perfect in every way, and any problems or concerns we had challenged our perfection. We knew that our children's behaviour was different and that these differences were rooted in their past, but we were too inexperienced as parents and too lacking in confidence to demand that our children's needs be taken seriously. The overriding response we obtained was one of trying to ignore our children's difference and thus their and our needs. It took a lot of confidence in ourselves as parents and a lot of research to understand and discuss the issues, challenge this response, and develop ways for our children to express their experiences and pain.

Adoption is different. It's great, it's wonderful, my children fill my universe – *but we are different and so are our needs!*

CHAPTER 3

Adopting Babies and Toddlers

It used to be the adoption dream – a healthy, normal baby who could become 'one of your own'. Babies for adoption were seen as parentless children without the baggage of long, unhappy histories of abuse and grief, and the trauma of feeling unwanted.

Abortion laws and the change in society's attitude to single parents has meant that today the number of people wanting to adopt a baby far exceeds the number of babies needing new families. Few agencies will now consider adoptive parents who are not prepared to take a 'baby' up to the age of two. Even if you are accepted as a potential adopter for this age group the wait can be long. But baby adoptions do happen – there are about a thousand in Britain every year. However, they are not always the easy option that they were once perceived to be.

'A baby or toddler doesn't have the skills to articulate their feelings verbally. The child is still being uprooted but has no voice to ask why,' said one adopter of two babies. 'Just because you have adopted a baby it doesn't mean that you can assume it has no feelings about what went before.'

Adoptive parents of babies tell stories of babies that don't like to be cuddled and babies that don't smile. Because of the trauma of being separated – even when only a few weeks old – from their birth parents, adopted babies may later develop a range of childhood problems.

Those families that do adopt babies are increasingly understanding the importance of bonding with this tiny new member of the family. 'I never let anyone else feed my adopted baby or change her nappies. It was important that the baby knew who I was and this was how to tell her,' said one adoptive mother. Others have gone one step further and have succeeded in breastfeeding or at least suckling their adopted babies in order to help create the physical and emotional bond all babies need in order to develop normally.

Even then, niggling at the back of many adoptive parent's minds, is the question: 'How can I be sure I will love this child as much as one I might have given birth to?'

Here are a few stories of the joy – and sometimes the pain – of adopting a baby.

● ● ●

Worth all the waiting

Four years ago, after lengthy fertility investigations, I was told that it was unlikely that I would ever become pregnant again due to an untreated infection following the birth of my daughter. We approached a local voluntary adoption agency. Our home study was rewarding and brought us much closer together.

We heard about a little boy of two who needed a placement. Very excited, we both went for our medicals. However, my husband was found to have a minor condition, which caused the agency's doctor some concern. A month before we were due to go to panel, our case was deferred for a year. It was a bombshell. We cried, we were angry, but life went on and we didn't give up.

Our GP kept a regular check on my husband's condition. He eventually said it was his belief that nothing would change this condition. He wrote to the agency's doctor telling him this and telling them that he thought we would make good adoptive parents.

Several months later our social worker phoned. 'I've good news, the agency's doctor agrees with yours and she is recommending that your case goes to panel as soon as possible.' We were accepted.

It was nearly a year later that we were told about a little boy, who was then nearly a year old. Shortly afterwards we were told that the panel had chosen us to be his parents. We will never forget that day – we were in shock.

I cannot describe our feelings when the day arrived for us to meet our son. We spent a whole week travelling over 200 miles daily to see him and spend time with him, all four of us getting to know each other. Day by day it became harder to leave him at his foster home.

Although we had spent many hours during our home study discussing our feelings, nothing could have prepared us for the strength of the emotions we felt when we brought him home.

The support we receive from our families and friends is amazing. Other people's reactions also surprise us. People I hardly know stop me in the village and admire my beautiful baby, who is now 18 months old and a bundle of mischief. People who haven't met him ask: 'Is he English or did you go to Romania?' Like so many others, they do not realise that there are English children needing adoptive parents.

We are all delighted; we wallow in the pleasure our little boy gives us, laugh at his antics, cherish the abundant love he has to give and love him dearly in return. Most of all, we give thanks that in this world full of anger, war, death and deep recession, the arrival of our son reminded us of the things that really matter in life.

We waited so long because this little boy was meant for us and we were meant for him.

A baby straight from hospital

'I'm sorry, you are not going to be able to have children.' After five years of marriage those were the words my husband and I heard from our doctor. We were devastated.

After a couple of days, having decided that we really did want children, we tried to find out about how to adopt. We were totally unprepared for all the problems and disappointments to be faced down this road. However, we were finally accepted by an independent Christian adoption society in London. We were told we would be able to adopt a baby, although perhaps not a very young one.

I personally could not prepare myself in any practical way – I couldn't buy any baby clothes or things like a pram or a cot. I couldn't cope with attending the antenatal-type classes I have heard advocated for adoptive parents; I was still feeling raw and not fully able to believe that I was going to have a baby.

After a year of waiting we had a phone call telling us that we had been chosen to have a baby who would be born within the next few days. We were over the moon: this was more than we had ever hoped for. We would be taking the baby from the hospital; no one else would have had him.

The society told us they would phone again within the next few days, once the baby had been born. The days turned into a week and then a fortnight – the baby must be overdue. I was frantic. At last the phone call came: it was a boy, everything was fine and could we fetch him in five to ten days time? The morning after we had another call asking us if we could come straight away, as we could bring him home at once. We panicked. I phoned my mother and she and a friend went out and practically bought out the local baby shop. We picked up some things from her on the long journey to the hospital. The trip took eight hours and every mile of the way we were excited and scared in turn.

We finally arrived at the hospital and were at last led into the room where our little precious baby boy was sleeping. We were allowed to stay overnight at the hospital, where the nurses told me when to feed and change him. The thing I remember most about that first sleepless night (there were many to follow) was feeding my baby and changing him, being soaked and wondering where the 'water' was coming from.

Our little boy was checked over by a doctor the next morning and then we were on our way. He was two and a half days old.

I was so grateful to have been given so young a baby. We had no chance to see him or get used to him. I felt like any other new mother having to accept her baby, healthy or not. He had not got used to a name, he had no routine. I could do it all.

Our second child was only five weeks old when we had her and I felt the loss of those few weeks, having had our first child practically from birth.

Breastfeeding adopted babies

After 19 operations in less than ten years, including IVF and a multiple pregnancy, we decided enough was enough and set off down the road of adoption. Our local agency took us on and we were approved for a baby under 12 months old.

Gosh, pregnant by proxy, licensed to shop as of the approval date – there was no stopping me. I began 'nesting'. I made bedding and cot bumpers, clothes, etc. I bought bits and bobs from here and there. I allowed myself a normal nine-month period of waiting before getting too anxious.

All through my wait I knew there was an area of infertility which troubled me – breastfeeding. I set about the mountainous task of discovering all I could. When my husband and I discussed it we both felt that I was strong enough emotionally to take it on but that it must not be looked at in terms of amount of milk made – just purely in terms of closeness of body contact. Some people were aghast and some said it wasn't possible. We advised our social worker and she was supportive, as were my doctor and health visitor.

I was told that a baby had been born and we were matched with her. I rushed out and hired a pump from the National Childbirth Trust. I pumped every two hours for ten minutes each side. I developed no real soreness and one Sunday evening I saw the first drops of milk. As it happened, the following day was D-Day.

We visited that night and saw our beautiful baby girl for the first time. I wanted her that minute but had to wait until the following day before I could hold her. We saw her the next morning at the foster mother's house. I can never describe the hours of that morning adequately. We took her home and after letting her settle in for a few days I began to offer her my breast. It took her a little while but soon she loved to suckle. The breast became her haven in times of trouble; it never failed to placate and ease her. She and I derived so much pleasure that any description would be inadequate. Sadly, at three and a half months she discovered THE THUMB and never liked to suckle after that. She is now 15 months old, we are very close, and she is a bright and securely attached child.

Baby placements are not always straightforward

When talking about adoption, people often assume that those who adopt young infants will have a relatively trouble-free ride and that it is the adopters of children with special needs who are likely to have problems. However, not all straightforward baby placements work out smoothly and problems may arise many years after a baby is placed. We have had three baby placements and while the younger child is fairly easy, both the older children have their problems.

Our son Philip was a six-week-old healthy baby when he came to us. He was lovely, if extremely wriggly and lively. When he was two he was joined by a demanding nine-month-old sister, but it was not until he was three that he began to get increasingly irritable, aggressive and sometimes violent. The years from four to eight were dominated by Philip's overactivity. The other things we find difficult to cope with are his totally chaotic personality and his disobedience; he loses everything and is quite unable to organise himself for going to school, swimming, etc. It can be almost impossible to get him to fit in with family plans, come to wash, go to bed, etc. Philip is very self-centred and unaware of other people and their needs.

This sounds negative, but there are plenty of good bits in between. Philip is always good in company or on holiday. He is a marvellous outdoor child and will be happy for hours on a mountain or a beach. He has a lovely sense of humour and can be affectionate. Philip is a 'stroboscope' child, changing from light to dark and back again rapidly and unpredictably.

Our second child Louise lived with her natural mother until she was five months old and then in an excellent foster home until she was nine months old before coming to us. She was terrified and clung to me like a little monkey, and I carried her around on my left hip for several months. I couldn't put her down for a second; she even had to sit on my knee on the loo! She awoke at 5.30 every morning and started screaming. At first, she couldn't bear my husband to be in the same room as us.

Gradually, the clinging and the disturbed behaviour decreased, until by the time she was three I felt she was fairly normal. Unfortunately, at this stage my mother, who lives some distance from us, became ill. I started staying with her for one week a month, taking only the baby and leaving Philip and Louise in the good care of my husband and a kind neighbour. Louise became impossible, morose, rejecting, demanding and insanely jealous of the baby. I left them five or six times; Philip turned not a hair but Louise hasn't recovered yet and remains desperately insecure. There is no way I can leave her with the trolley at the supermarket checkout. Louise said to me recently: 'As soon as I can't see you, I think someone is going to kidnap me.' As far as she is concerned she was kidnapped twice before she was one! A few weeks ago I made the bad mistake of leaving her at her ballet class for about 40 minutes. Through sheer bad luck she found that I was not in my usual place in the waiting room and when I came back she was weeping, with a swollen face and a pounding heart, and her hands shook so much she could hardly get dressed. She knows that at nearly nine she should not need me to wait for her but this was a physiological panic reaction that she could not control. We hope that with time, patience and love she will gain the independence appropriate to her age.

What of Isobel, our third child? She turned not a hair when she came to us at 7 months. She is sunny, cuddly, loving and quite straightforward most of the time. She is extremely normal.

We were lucky to get three babies. It has its problems – but I wouldn't swap them now for all the tea in China.

Answering a birth mother's questions

The ten months between our initial enquiry and being approved by the adoption panel seemed endless. Had they forgotten about us? Were we unsuitable parents – despite our love of children? Had the letter of approval gone missing? Would we ever hear from the agency again?

Approval by the panel brought delight, but being selected for a placement by an unknown mother somewhere in the South of England a few months later brought even greater excitement. From that time on, the process of adoption became far more 'open'. Opportunities arose to exchange a list of suggested names for the unborn baby, and tentative preparations for a possible meeting with Jane in the not too distant future were made.

The phone rang one Saturday evening and an unfamiliar voice brought the news that we had so longed for. The baby had arrived. He was a healthy baby boy weighing 7lb 4oz, and we were to meet him and his birth mother.

Meeting Jane, Ben's birth mother, was unforgettable. We sympathised with her as she, a 19-year-old student, gave away the most treasured possession of her young life. We felt great pangs of guilt and shared the anguish that she was suffering.

Would we care for young Ben? Would we tell him about her? Would we raise him in a Christian home where true Biblical values were respected and honoured? Would we love and support him through thick and thin? These were some of Jane's concerns, and none of our efforts to reassure her lessened our sense of remorse for taking him away from her.

We hugged and wept together as we realised that this might be a once-in-a-lifetime encounter.

Emotions ran high, too, in the hospital ward where we set eyes on Ben for the very first time. Needless to say, he was the most special baby in the world. How could we reject him? How could we not care for him? The wait had been so worthwhile and a new chapter in our lives together was about to unfold.

Culture clashes

When our two new sons joined us they were aged four and two. They came to us from a 'short-term' foster home, where they had lived for 16 months, well looked after and loved. Even so, there were some culture clashes – or perhaps 'gaps' would be a more suitable word.

For example, they had little experience of going to the park, and would sink with exhaustion murmuring '[t]ired, [t]ired' practically the moment we left the car. They liked the swings but had no idea what to do with the small climbing frame, wandering underneath it in bewilderment. In desperation, after several fruitless visits, I had to climb it myself, exhorting, explaining and guiding feet. Now, of course, they climb anything and everything confidently, while I worry about them falling! Taken on picnics, they threw paper wrappers onto the ground robustly and were clearly amazed when I insisted we collect the rubbish to take home.

Our main problem, however, was communication. Their speech was unclear – they generally omitted the first and often the last consonants of each word – and since we'd moved to London from the North, their accents were very different from ours. Those early anxious days were made more difficult and frustrating for all of us when I failed, again and again, to understand. I managed to work most things out eventually – but by then the moment had passed.

These were minor difficulties of course, and time soon resolved them. The children were so young that they settled very quickly and now, nearly two years later, I'm glad to say that we all feel very much part of the same family.

A positive start

In September we were approved to adopt up to two children under the age of five – although the panel felt we could cope with three.

The following March we heard about a baby boy aged nine months, but didn't allow ourselves to feel hopeful at all and told no one about it. In May we were amazed to hear that he had been freed for adoption and that, out of three couples, we were the ones chosen.

A week later we met our son for the first time; he was now eleven and a half months old and had been with his foster family since the age of four months. As soon as we walked in, a photo of an older brother was thrust into our hands by his social worker: 'This is what he'll be like at ten!' We had hardly been able to take in the cheeky, grinning toddler hanging onto the sofa. For the hour we were there he was totally hyperactive, and I became completely manic. I was already feeling overwhelmed by the enormity of the change in his and our lives.

I spent the next few days in tears. Why had we ever put ourselves into the position of having to make such a decision? I had expected to feel instant love and I didn't. On the other hand, I drew strength from my husband's confident serenity – he was already glowing. Perhaps foolishly, I voiced some of my fears to the social workers, who then told the foster mother that she hadn't allowed me to mother him enough in that hour's visit! We saw him again at the end of the week and I felt much happier and calmer.

Our two-week introduction began in mid-June and was a wonderful time. There were many sunny days, so we were able to go out a lot; the foster family were brilliant and our son adapted very well. By the end of the two weeks he was as happy in our arms as theirs. On the move-in day the foster parents brought him over, had lunch and left with an exchange of letters and tears. Since then they have continued to be close friends, and his foster father is now his godfather.

In January of the next year we applied to adopt our son, but by then his birth mother's circumstances had changed and she contested the adoption. This caused the process to take a year and to be quite worrying for us. It was a great relief when she consented just before the final hearing 13 months later. When I excitedly called out the good news to my husband and son in the garden, my son said: 'I think Mummy's found chocolate money!' Our second son moved in a year later aged five and a half months.

Our sons are now both in primary school, doing well and have good friendships. The older one still throws major tantrums which we try to deal with in a variety of ways; outside of these both boys are affectionate and warm with an abundance of energy. Both talk rarely but openly about their adoptions. I'm still the one who looks after their life story books most.

So far, family life has been as would be expected – tiring, mostly fun and happy. Our boys are lucky enough to have always been loved, and although we know there will be lots of questions to answer we hope the love they have experienced will create a strong foundation from which they can grow.

CHAPTER 4
Adopting Schoolchildren

Most people will tell you that this is just what you don't want to do: adopt children who feel rejected and dejected, and are emotionally traumatised by the lack of ordinary, caring, loving parents.

Schoolchildren are old enough to have clear memories and confused loyalties and habits. These are the children that carry a lot of emotional baggage that will be unravelled in the years to come on your living room floor. It is baggage that you and they will always have to carry. They often know who their birth parents are and just what has happened.

These children's smiling faces fill the pages of Adoption UK's quarterly journal. They hope that someone will want to 'take them home' but are all too aware of how unwanted they are. Their self-esteem is often non-existent. They have probably spent their short lives being uprooted and pushed from pillar to post. They have been let down by life and are instinctively distrustful of any offer of permanence. Their emotions are like a basket of brittle eggshells.

And despite all the love offered by an adoptive parent, inside they often suffer from a divided sense of loyalty, wanting against all the odds to defend the parents who gave birth to them.

For adoptive parents, taking on older, school-age children is a giant challenge – a stormy rescue operation. And as they go to the rescue, parents have to come to terms with the inalterables. First and foremost, they are never going to know the whole story. Their adopted child is like a puzzle with lots of missing pieces; as the years pass many of the missing pieces may be found and filled in – but a few will remain permanently and sometimes purposefully 'lost'.

Adoptive parents also have to accept that they might never love these adopted children in the same way as they love children born to them or think they might have loved a child born to them. They must know that it is okay to love these children equally but differently.

Adopters of older children often find that they take on not one child but an instant family of two or three brothers and sisters at the same time.

If the adopters and adoptees are well matched, the rewards for all can be enormous. Children can be seen to blossom and grow, physically and emotionally; to take pride in themselves where once they had none. Transformations of all sorts take place. 'The girls [eight and ten] could hardly read and write when they came to us 18 months ago, but now they even keep books in the loo,' said one adoptive parent.

Another describes the moment she really became 'mum' to her adopted son. 'The breakthrough can be very long in coming but the emotional return is enormous. Like the day he gave me my first Mother's Day card.'

• • •

The silver lining

Our first adoption was that of Pip. He was placed at ten months, lively and trusting, but undersized and 'wise beyond his years'. We realised we were in for a very short honeymoon period when, within the first week, he gnawed through three armchairs and started eating the earth out of the pot plants.

Pip was a German Shepherd cross: big, furry, licky, always under your feet, and a trial to the patience of a saint (the social worker's view, and she didn't have to live with him). Luckily, the social worker took the view that people mad enough to keep an animal after having had to repair the sofa 14 times must be tolerant and able to cope with the upheaval of adoption.

So we found ourselves going to meet two sisters aged nine and six with a view to adopting them. We'd been warned beforehand that the nine-year-old's past experiences meant that, whilst placement would probably work, she'd never be able to get physically close to me, her new dad. We played in the park with them and both girls demanded that I carry them back to their foster mum's – and that was after the six-year-old had cheeked me and been dumped in the park litter bin for her pains.

At the girls' school we were told that the six-year-old was bright but the nine-year-old was not. They'd kindly kept her informed of their views, notably that she wouldn't be able to read, so why bother? This didn't do much for her already weak self-confidence. This extended to all her activities, and we watched askance as she sauntered along the track in the running race at school sports, predictably coming in last.

The foster mum had done a great job of preparing the girls. Without her support, common sense and encouragement, things would have been much hairier than they actually were.

We were lucky enough to forge tremendous relationships with both the girls' new schools. With regular meetings to exchange ideas, we appear to have been able to create the environment the eldest needed. From being unable to read four years ago, she now not only reads but is in the top few in her year at high school in virtually every subject. What made us most proud was seeing her in the school sports in her middle school winning the 200 metres against a much taller girl in a determined race for the line.

Apart from a love of books, the youngest has discovered music – a love she shares with me. It has been a great time of discovery for us all, not the same but akin to the firsts that all parents enjoy. The first successful music exam, the first netball match won, the first instance of throwing up after lights out (Mount Vesuvius has nothing on a nine-year-old who's bolted her food), the first time carrying the Brownie Guide flag at church parade – they're all special moments in their own way.

I'm not saying it's all been sweetness and light. We still have those occasions when the doubts crowd in, but in each case we come back to the conclusion that our communication as a family is good.

The girls are definitely here for good – for better rather than worse.

Are we growing onions or roses?

I have been to many therapy sessions since my daughter, then aged eight and a half, arrived four years ago. All have used the onion analogy to explain how to help both myself and my daughter come to terms with problems which are rooted in our past.

This 'onion' therapy assumes that we have papered over things in our past which have affected us adversely, such as an overprotective mother or, in the extreme, sexual abuse. In order to stop these things affecting us we need to carefully peel back the layers of adversity to get to the root of the problem and come to terms with it. This is peeling back the layers of the onion.

Until recently I accepted this as a very necessary if painful exercise, which would help my daughter grow into adulthood without the traumas of her past life affecting her behaviour and relationships. But if you peel onions you get tears and more tears, until the onion becomes a smaller onion.

I asked myself, 'Why am I doing this? Do I need more tears?' I have come to the conclusion that, like so many therapies and practices which may work for others, the onion doesn't work for us. We need a different approach.

Hence the rose.

I am parenting a fragile rosebud which one day is going to grow into a rose. At this point in time, it's one of those rosebuds that has developed too early in the year. (She has had to grow up too quickly and often seems more like an 18-year-old than a 13-year-old because of the abuse she has suffered.)

My rosebud has been affected by the frost and has some brown edges on her petals; she seems to have a lot of thorns but not many leaves to her stem, and her stem seems very thin. (It is easy to be hurt by her if you approach her in the wrong way; at other times she is fragile and vulnerable.)

Although the sun is now shining and she has been given plenty of food, water, care and attention, my rosebud does not want to open her petals to reveal the beautiful rose beneath. (It is almost as if she is afraid to grow up and is refusing to accept responsibility for herself or for her actions; she continually denies that she is secure and safe and in a normal family, and is often looking for ways of staying a child.)

We have all seen rose bushes with rosebuds which have been damaged by a frost. Some never blossom into roses; others (given extra attention and protection from greenfly) will do eventually. The rose may not be perfect, and may still have brown edges to the petals, but it will look and smell like a rose, and will delight and give pleasure. My daughter responds to understanding, love, support and security, and by listening to how she feels and what she needs I believe I can help her to blossom and become an adult – perhaps not a perfect adult, but she needs to know that none of us are. To try to be perfect is to be doomed to failure, but to accept ourselves and others with the blemishes and odd faults we have is success indeed.

Reflections

Never had a pair of eyes pierced me so completely. Yours are very blue, large, round and disconcertingly unblinking; you have just told me how it feels to know no trust. You are 12 years old – in many respects as careworn as a man of 50 and yet inclined, whenever possible, to the reactions and indulgences of a five-year-old.

You have lived as our son for four and a half years, and in that time your father and I have understood so little, but witnessed such courage and tenacity that our view of the strength of the human personality has been changed beyond belief.

Those eyes, as you look at me now, remind me of that most memorable of all days when we first met. At seven, you were so small and knock-kneed and yet so penetrating. We were so nervous, anxious to please and apprehensive as to how we would meet up to your initial expectations of 'forever' parents. Within seconds your glance appraised us, but then you were well practised in the art of measuring up adults, having by this time already lived within the care of eight different sets of carers. The odd thing is that superficially you always seemed such a trusting boy, so ready to hug, kiss, and tell; how wrongly we all assessed you.

When you first moved into our house it all seemed too easy. Sharing, jealousy and piecing your history together were to be expected as problems;

with these we coped. Wet beds and trousers were an irritation which slowly you have almost left behind.

We were lucky to have lots of support and opportunities to consider varying explanations. I remember when we visited a friend and you served pretend tea in plastic cups to all the adults. No one showed embarrassment at your age-inappropriate behaviour. In my memory it's clearly etched as one of those steps along the road of adjusting to being the mother of a child with a long and hidden history. We just did not realise how very much you had missed.

Of lies, you have been the master; once started you would tell any number rather than acknowledge the original misdeed or omission. How angry we have been. Forgive us child, we had no understanding of how early in life you learnt to believe you were bad and to trust only yourself. For you, it seems, the truth was life-threatening if a misdeed was known; you and your plastic bag of belongings, you believed, would be moved to the next frightening and bewildering place.

In your ninth year, nights before your adoption hearing, you shared with your father and sister the terror of believing that any minute now a social worker would come to move you before the judge had agreed to your stay. While waiting for your hearing, you panicked on finding yourself alone in a marbled gents' cloakroom; you screamed, believing there was still time for your fate to be changed.

Your mum had agreed to your adoption, but six months after the hearing you asked to see your mum and check that it was okay. It was a harrowing experience. You showed your mum your life story and chatted; quietly and decisively you then called it to a close, satisfied, it appeared, that mum knew and did not mind. It took another 18 months of ups and downs to brave the next terrifying question: 'How could she be happy to have given me away?'

Always, when open to sharing, in your rare moments of being relaxed, you are intelligent and poised.

Oh little boy, how enormous your aloneness has felt, how isolating the responses of ourselves and your teachers must have seemed. How inappropriate to call you 'naughty'.

I am sure that one day soon now remembering will no longer bring you dragons. The truth will stop being a threat. At last, before it's all too late, childhood will begin to be yours.

The icing on the cake

When we were first told about our family (three siblings aged five months, 18 months and five years), we were told by their social worker that the eldest little girl was a 'can of worms'. Emotionally abused before she came into care, she was then placed in a foster home where, unlike her younger siblings, she didn't fit in and wasn't wanted. Her foster parents described her as a deceitful, naughty child – a 'time bomb waiting to go off'. This only drew us closer to her and when we finally met this 'time bomb' we saw a little girl masquerading as an old lady and crying out to be loved. She had no self-respect, would do or say anything to start an argument and didn't really trust anyone.

Of course, the first few months were hard; we had sessions of either wailing or staring, she would play one parent off against the other, and she regressed completely. She was constantly insisting that it was a baby we wanted and had to be reassured that we loved and wanted all of them. She wouldn't let us cuddle her, couldn't say goodbye to anyone, and kissing anyone, including us, was definitely a no-go area. Physically, it was like having three children under two; emotionally, it was like having six!

But the rewards are enormous – the first time she called us mummy and daddy, when we got a giggle rather than a stare for telling her she was pretty, when she told us it was she we had longed for, and when she started wanting to do all the 'normal' things seven-year-olds do.

To see the joy that shines from her now gives us great joy, and in contrast to what most people expected, she returns our love threefold. Our other two also give us much love and joy, and have caused us some headaches in spite of their youth at placement. Anyone considering adoption who talks to us now and says they would love to have children placed as young as possible is told: 'It is our eldest who has given us the greatest pleasure.' We would certainly adopt a disruptive five-year-old again…and probably will.

We didn't plan it this way…

Shortly after our marriage it was discovered that I was extremely unlikely to conceive. Having got over the shock and embarked unsuccessfully on some infertility treatment, we finally decided to adopt. We were told that we would not get a baby but planned to try for as young a child as possible, aged between 18 months and five years. Our social services department recommended that we foster first to 'prove' ourselves and learn what it was like to have a child around. We were approved as short-term foster parents for up to two children aged up to five years.

A call came and we were asked if we could take a boy of seven for about three months. He was described as violent, ESN ('educationally sub-normal') and unloveable. He had been in care for about six months with his younger sister and had been through two children's homes and three sets of foster parents. His current foster carers were washing their hands of him, but his sister was remaining with them. The plan was for him to have an intensive period of total care to prepare him for adoption. A very small, pale, anxious little boy walked over our doorstep, carrying a snooker table almost as big as himself.

During his first two weeks Peter had a couple of temper tantrums, but on each occasion we simply picked him up, put him in his room and told him that we didn't want to see him until he was over his silliness. We never had another tantrum.

As time passed he began to perform very well at his special day school, and his teachers said he might even reach the point at which he could be described as being 'of low intelligence'. His social worker was having trouble finding suitable adoptive parents for him, so we kept him for another three months and then a further three months. By now he was very much part of our lives and our family. We formally applied to adopt him, and that was when some of our problems started.

Initially, he was very excited and happy about becoming a permanent part of our family. Then he became confused as to why he was not going back to his mother. He decided that as I loved him and wanted him it must be my fault, and stopped speaking to me, started wetting, stopped eating and generally looked very pale and miserable. He knew he wanted his new daddy and his new house, lifestyle and friends, but he wanted his birth mum as well. Eventually, with the help of a very skilful social worker, he accepted the problems his birth mother had and settled back into a normal routine.

After his great improvement at school it had been decided to transfer him to the special needs class of our local junior school. He loved his new school and was soon transferred from the special needs class to a normal mainstream peer group.

Then came the day of the court case. It was fiercely contested but eventually all went well. Peter came home laughing, singing and clapping his hands. This lasted for two months. Then the reaction set in and he became once again pale and withdrawn, wetting and soiling. This was the infamous 'testing' time, when he wanted to see if we really meant it and would send him back if he was really awful. It seemed horrendous at the time, but we all came through it and are now back on a reasonably even keel. Peter has even been officially recognised as a gifted child, especially in maths and science (so much for ESN).

Peter has now been with us for two years. We have all had some rocky moments, and I am sure there are more to come as we slowly wear away his insecurities and build up his own feelings of self-worth. He has made enormous strides and brought us great joy, pride and happiness – as well as a few sleepless nights. Life is working out so well that we are currently applying to adopt another child of school age. Having started off convinced that we could only cope with a pre-school child, we have seen for ourselves that Peter is exactly right for us.

The turning point

Our eldest son was seven years old at placement and had been in care for nearly four years, mostly in a children's home, where he was well on the way to being institutionalised.

Initially he was very mistrusting, and was determined to just 'use' us until he decided that he'd had enough. He wouldn't allow us to touch him, especially me (the mother figure), or show him any kind of affection. He was extremely attention-seeking and demanded our time constantly. He was afraid of the dark and of being left. Eventually and slowly, very slowly, after a lot of love and care expressed physically and verbally, constantly and consistently, he began to respond, but still he wouldn't show any emotion. The turning point was the day I broke down and cried in front of him because I didn't know what else to do and he cried with me. From then on he started to regress, but only in the home; outside he was 'normal', although he still gravitated to playing with children a year or two younger than himself. It was only much later, when my second son was placed with us at 16 months, that I realised just how far he had regressed. He was always hanging on to my skirt and followed me everywhere, even the loo! He sat on my knee for cuddles at every opportunity, even at breakfast time. He wanted to be carried to bed like a baby. I had to support his head and place him in bed on his side. Once, I even improvised a nappy out of a towel.

This period didn't last for ever: by the time he was adopted at ten it was all in the past and he was a happy, popular and quite balanced boy. His adoption order was granted without a hitch. My son timed how long we were in with the judge and it was less than two minutes.

Then and now

In October 1974 the Adoption UK Journal carried the following details of two children: 'Thomas and George are brothers aged nine years and six years respectively. They have both been in the same children's home since 1969 and it is essential that they be offered a long-term foster home together, with a view to adoption. Both boys are very attractive, Thomas being half-Chinese, George being half-African. Thomas is an intelligent child, a typically lively and mischievous boy who is easy to get on with. He enjoys school and outside activities like the Cubs. He is not a troublesome child, although he is naturally intelligent like his brother. Both boys are loveable and they need a stable home where they would receive plenty of love, patience and understanding.'

At that time we had a family of five, three who had been born to us, then aged nine and a half, eight and five, and two who had been adopted as babies who were then two and a half and 11 months old. We had decided we had room for one more and were looking for an older boy, by which we meant a boy somewhere between two and five years old. Two more of the age of Thomas and George was definitely not what we had in mind.

But I couldn't put them out of my mind, and kept rereading their details and pouring over their photographs. It gradually dawned on me that they were exactly the boys we wanted, and that they would fit into the family very well. I wrote a long letter, well aware that we might not be the type of family they were looking for. I tried to anticipate what they would see as our shortcomings in order to forestall a negative response. We were told that their authority was assessing a childless couple for the boys, but that if this fell through they would get back to us. We had to be content with this and put our emotions 'on hold'. Nevertheless, our older children continued to discuss who would sleep where and how big a pudding I would have to cook in future.

In the event, and at the end of a long process, Thomas and George joined our family in the autumn of 1975. We then had children of 11, ten, nine, seven, six, three and two years old. Looking back, I cannot believe how much energy I must have had. My youngest daughter, who is now 24 and herself the mother of two small girls, says, 'Whatever you were on at the time, Mum, I wish I could have some!'

There were the usual understatements and omissions in the boys' profiles. The 'difficulties' with schooling were extreme, and there was no mention of the asthma that one of them suffered from, thankfully now outgrown, but causing quite serious problems for many years. There were difficult behaviour problems too, and much time and energy had to be spent on making sure each one of the seven children had their physical and emotional needs attended to.

The boys' mother had died before social services started to look for a new family for them, and neither father had been much involved in their lives. Thomas, who did some searching of his own when he was grown-up, has met a great uncle, spoken on the phone to a cousin, and has a copy of his mother's birth certificate and her parents' marriage certificate. George has never shown any interest in his background, preferring, as he puts it, to look forward rather than backward. But of course, he can share in what Thomas has found out.

Thomas and George are now aged 31 and 28. They are both in full-time work, own cars and are buying their own homes. Thomas and his girlfriend live together and George is at present footloose and fancy-free, working abroad most of the year. On his most recent trip home he recorded a small part in a popular television series, which we look forward to seeing. A new career move, perhaps?

You can never know exactly how a family is going to develop, even when they are all biologically related to each other, and some of our extended family and friends watched us anxiously in the early years. It wasn't all plain sailing, but we don't regret doing it. The children, no longer children, are all close. They'll be around for each other long after we've gone, and that's one of the most satisfying aspects of the whole thing.

A very professional beginning

It took exactly two years from our first decision to start a family for our two children, aged seven and eight, to move in. Contrary to stories I have heard about 'vetting' for adoption, we experienced a straightforward and helpful preparation period.

Our hopes of conceiving naturally were dashed within six months, typical symptoms of menopause being confirmed by a blood test. Our GP was the first understanding professional; he said he was 'gobsmacked' by the diagnosis and 'would rather tell someone they had cancer than this'. I was relieved it was 'only' infertility, not cancer.

Then we started to make enquiries to adoption agencies. We contacted three local social services departments and two independent agencies within our area. Each agency had a different agenda. One said, 'Write to us again in six months if you're still interested.' Another lectured us on the importance of same-race placements, but concluded that they 'even had a white child placed with black foster parents'. The third implied that we were rushing into our decision and had not grieved adequately for our infertility. Both the others were positive, friendly and helpful, and we settled on the one that promised to get going soonest.

It was useful to consider two sets of children in parallel, as it helped us to identify our priorities and anxieties. We told each set of social workers that we were considering the others. Likewise, they made it clear that other couples had expressed interest in the children. Everybody seemed helpful and honest with us, and ready to supply further information as we requested it.

Billy and Ian had an equally disturbed past, including severe neglect and multiple abuse, but were receiving considerable therapy and had been in excellent (separate) placements for the last couple of years. At last the telephone call came. Billy and Ian's social workers wanted to proceed with the placement. By then everybody was off on holiday, exactly when each was needed for a crucial decision or signature. We thought we might get the children before the end of the summer term: no way!

We were both terribly nervous before the meeting, but the children put us at our ease immediately. They were just as we expected and we had a glorious afternoon playing and talking together. The two-month programme of introductory meetings was meticulously arranged; each meeting was longer than the last and there was a gradual transfer of responsibility, with therapy sessions and reviews before the final move was fixed. Farewells were all planned, including the complications of us collecting both children from school.

The day of the move went very smoothly for us, with lots of photos, warm goodbyes and assurances that everybody was only a phone call away. Billy actually had a headache and temperature from the stress of the event, but Ian could hardly believe that his dream had come true. The car was full of sacks of teddies, boxes of cards and life story records, and cases of summer clothes – plus a bicycle on a hastily purchased roof carrier.

Billy and Ian have now been with us for seven weeks. There is obviously a lot of hard work ahead for the four of us in learning to live together as a family and in coming to terms with their difficult past. But we have confidence in the medical, social work and educational support we have received so far. We are optimistic that we are the right parents for the boys and that they are the right children for us.

At last I had become a mum

When I look at my son sleeping in his bed, I can't really believe that he is mine. All the years of waiting and hoping to become a mum have at last ended.

I stand there and think back to the time I was told that I would never become a mother naturally and that IVF was my only hope. The sorrow and pain of that moment is still there in my heart – but a hope had been placed, so off I went on the IVF trail. We had four attempts in all, and of course each one failed. I won't go into details, but anyone who has been through it will know the pain (and cost!) involved.

We started on the road to approval and, thank goodness, it was much more pleasant than IVF: in fact, we both quite enjoyed it. It was really nice to be with couples who were childless like ourselves and the group really bonded, with us all becoming friends.

I read about Danny in the British Agencies for Fostering and Adoption (BAAF) news-sheet *Focus on Fives* and thought he sounded like just the child for us.

I remember well the first time we saw Danny, a little boy with blond curly hair and green eyes. I had hoped that I would feel instant love for him, but of course, I didn't. Strangely, my big, burly husband did.

Then the time came to take Danny home with us, and that day was a day to remember, because at last I had become a mum. I kept looking at this little boy running madly around our house opening cupboards and drawers, and generally having a good nose around his new home. I kept thinking, 'He is ours, we've done it, we have become parents.' It was a dream come true: now I was like everyone else, I wasn't a childless woman any more, I was a mum.

I knew that from then on my life was going to change completely, but it was a change that I had dreamed of for 12 years.

I have to say that it hasn't all been sweetness and light, and I did cry quite a lot in the first two months. I couldn't work out whether they were tears of joy or sadness, but, whatever the reason, shedding them made me feel better. Every day is different: I never know what Danny is going to do or say next.

I don't know whether we have been particularly lucky in our adoption, because Danny seems to have bonded with us straight away. Perhaps there are more couples like us who, because they are having such a good time being families, don't feel the need to write about it.

But whether we are especially blessed or not, all I know is that I feel contented with my life and that we have a wonderful son who brings love into our lives. When he says, 'Mummy, I love you', I know that life doesn't get any better than this.

CHAPTER 5

Taking on an Adolescent

Not a child and not yet an adult: adolescents are going through difficult, emotionally challenging pre-teen and teenage years.

Adopting an adolescent is by no means easy. Stories of crashed cars, lying, stealing and police arrests abound from understanding but often necessarily leather-skinned adoptive parents. These young people, many of whom are streetwise and world-weary before they reach their teenage years, can't believe that you might find them worth the effort of loving, and can test you till breaking point. It takes time for them to accept that you might want them, love them, and be prepared to give them the last shot at family life that they need. These are 'high-risk' adoptions, but the rewards can be astonishing.

'To see a child feel sufficiently secure to be able to think positively about his future is an enormous reward,' said one adopter. 'And perhaps what people don't believe is how much love these teenagers have to give.'

Their past is never an open book to you. They carry it with them and often need to know and see a wide variety of members of their birth families – not just the one or two that a younger child might have selected or had selected for them. And they are of sufficient age to see who they want – old friends, old family and old contacts – and to do so with or without their adopters' permission. The choice of contact and where it takes place can be taken out of your hands.

There is also the problem of physical contact. You can't easily pick up a teenager and cuddle them on your lap for half an hour because they are upset, although a cuddle may be just what they need and want. They may have been subjected to inappropriate physical behaviour in their past, so you have to ensure you give them the right signals and that an innocent, affectionate hug is not misconstrued.

Another side of adopting a teenager is that it is often not just a test for you but also for your family and friends, some of whom will reel in horror at the thought of the arrival of this oversized cuckoo in your nest. 'You must be mad' is a common reaction to the announcement of an impending teenage adoption. 'It is when you find out who your real friends are,' said one adopter.

For these children childhood is almost over, and it is up to their adopters to give them some essence of what childhood is about and what it is to be a loved member of a supportive family. At the same time, the adopter is coping with all the natural adolescent angst that is flung at all parents of teenagers from time to time, but from a teenager who is as streetwise and world-weary as an adult twice their age and who has basic emotional insecurities and needs more commonly seen in a child less than half their age.

'All teenagers are in the process of becoming independent and detaching themselves from their families, but these teenagers are trying to attach and detach at the same time,' explained one adopter.

For many teenagers, finding the secure, loving family that has eluded them throughout their childhood is a priceless gift, though they may not say thank you and the seemingly unbelievable security of it may make them wish to test their new family to the limits. Their total lack of self-esteem, the result of having been pushed from pillar to post for much of their lives, can make them distrust the sincerity of your affection. 'Never give up,' says one successful adopter. Changes can take time and be painful; they have been graphically described by one experienced social worker as follows:

1. Walked down street – deep hole in the pavement – fell in.

2. Walked down street – deep hole in the pavement – fell in.

3. Walked down street – saw hole, but still fell in.

4. Walked down street – saw hole – walked round it.

5. Walked down another street.

It can be a very tough road and breakdowns do happen – but so do successes. Successful adopters of teenagers say that the key points are 'not to take most things too seriously' and 'not to be afraid to ask for help'.

• • •

Obnoxious but loveable

Our son was placed with us shortly before his fifteenth birthday last year. It has been a tiring 15 months, but also a very rewarding period in that we have seen such good progress in his emotional development. He is now like any 16-year-old: totally obnoxious but very loveable.

As a childless couple who have been married for 22 years, we felt that a lot of people thought (some actually said) that inexperienced parents taking on a teenager was a recipe for disaster. Our social worker has told us that we can now remove the L-plates. Although we know there is still a long way to go, we hope that once the adoption is completed we will have enough energy left to consider taking another child. We have come to realise how desperately the older children need families and how hard it is for social workers to place them. The rewards are tremendous when these young people begin to settle with their new family, and you feel a great sense of achievement. They have so much love to give, although it takes a long time for them to be able to show it.

Although this is a successful story, we can assure you we also go through extremely difficult times, when our son tests us to the limits. As adoptive parents we have found that during the difficult times a sense of humour helps enormously. It has been rewarding to see our son begin to progress at school and think about his future positively.

If we were asked what advice we would give to prospective adopters of teenage children it would be: never be afraid to ask for help from the placing agency; attend the support groups run by them, as you learn so much from other adoptive parents; and, most important of all, never give up.

You must be mad

'Poor thing.' 'Who, him or me?' 'You of course.' This was the spontaneous comment of the ten-year-old son of a friend when I announced we were planning to adopt a 13-year-old boy. He may have had his teenage sister in mind, as he then went on to say that a boy would probably be easier than a girl. We had various reactions, mainly along the lines of, 'You must be mad', or, 'You must be brave.' Maybe we were a bit of both, but perhaps our son was too; after all, it was as big a step for him as it was for us.

On the whole, people were sympathetic and interested. One friend had strong views against the whole idea of placing older children in families, and yet she made what has proved to be a very helpful comment: 'Don't take it too seriously.' At times when we have all been at odds with each other I have thought of this, and it really does help.

When we discussed our local support system during the assessment it sounded fine, but you win some, you lose some, and sometimes support turned up from unexpected quarters. We were lucky in knowing two local families, both of whom have adopted children now in their teens. Whatever our son has done, theirs has always gone one step further, so we feel we are doing all right. The children haven't really become friends – why should they? – but at first it was very important for our son to be able to say 'so and so is adopted'. Lately, he has said this far less often, which we believe and hope means he feels really well settled.

Gradually, our son has got to know half a dozen boys in the road, of different ages and at different schools. We are very fortunate in having a large field at the back of the house, and all the boys gather there to play football or tennis. We realise how much our son has grown-up when we remember how during that first summer he needed much encouragement to join the others. Last summer he needed much encouragement to leave his friends and come in to bed!

The support of other adopters and parents has been good. Sometimes it helps just to talk and sometimes they give useful advice. If you haven't been through the earlier years with a child you have missed out on a lot of basics, like where to go for football socks, trainers, etc.

Letter to a son

My dear son,

As we seem to find it very difficult at present to talk to each other without you threatening me with violence, I thought I would write to you.

As you know, I have been learning a lot about Attachment Disorder recently and it seems to me that your behaviour shows a lot of the signs of this. These include constantly telling lies, stealing and aggression.

One of the other things I have been told is that life is all about making choices. You make good choices and not-so-good choices. You know you have made good choices when good consequences happen – like when you go to college and you get your grant cheques, or when you ask me for something in a reasonable way and I give it to you.

You know when you have made wrong choices when bad consequences happen – like when you don't go to college and your grant cheque is cancelled, or when you tell me that if I don't give you what you want you will stab me or punch my cunt in and I refuse to give you what you want.

One of the things that I have learned is that making wrong choices is okay – that people make these choices because they have not learned enough to be able to make good choices.

You have often accused me of being overprotective, and you are probably right. I have shielded you from a lot of the bad consequences of the wrong choices you have made. I now realise this was wrong, and I will try hard in future to let you experience the consequences of all your actions.

I will be there to help you if you want, to listen to you and offer you support and encouragement for your good choices.

Regarding stealing and telling lies, when a person acts like this it is hard for other people to trust anything they say or do. Since I don't know whether any statement you make is the truth or a lie, I will decide for myself whether to believe you and act accordingly. If you decide that telling lies is not a good choice and start to act on this, please let me know so that I can decide whether to act differently myself.

Please remember that I love you, whether you make good or bad choices. Lots of luv, Mum XXX

To my darling daughter

My darling daughter, you have smashed into my world with your presence – I will never again be the same person. I am learning to love you as I learn to accept your ways and appreciate the colour you've brought into our family.

I was happy and contented with family life before you came; it was comfortable and unthreatening. In fact, I suppose it was too easy: I had found a nice rut which I feared to leave. Well, now I have been challenged by you in every area that others couldn't reach. I've resented you, hated the disturbance you've caused me, but wanted you for the sake of your beloved brother.

I've never had second thoughts about you. Since I first heard about you, I've always believed you were meant to be our daughter and always wanted you. I've wanted to love you so much, but love takes time to grow and we've had some pretty rough patches as we have started to get to know each other. I've wondered who is moulding who!

You've caused me such pain, and I'm sure you will again and again. I've grieved for the days in your life that we missed and for the influences we were not allowed to have on you in crucial times in your life. I've wished I could have been there for you when you were wounded by those who should have loved you more. I've wanted to suffer those wounds for you, prevent the marks they've made on your life, and save some of the innocence that you have lost in this cruel world.

I love your resilience. You have such pluck and fight. You are irrepressible and amazingly trusting. You have such impact and personality for one so small – you will always push the boundaries and challenge the world. In a way you have given me courage and restored my spirit of adventure. I love the way you've enriched our lives and broken down barriers. You have impacted on all our relationships, inside and outside the home and extended family. You are the source of such smiles and tears – you amaze us. You love yourself and have the self-confidence and assertiveness that I dream of!

What a transformation you've made in each of us. You are revolutionising our idea of physical affection, you even verbalise affection better than we do and you are more in tune with your feelings than we've ever been! You are a new concept in enjoying food, enjoying life and enjoying mess! We are learning what it is to be mother and father to a daughter – I pray we will be wise and loving and all we should be for you, with God's help.

I've enjoyed your admiration and adoration of your brother and your mutual tenderness and imagination.

You are lovely and beautiful and a precious gift – even if you can be rather prickly. I thank God for you, daughter. I hope we can grow up together as friends. We need each other, especially to rub off those prickles from each other. I hope we will be able to love and be loved as God intended, and have a good laugh!

Positive results

It's nine months now since my daughter was placed with me and just over a month since her adoption. I can't imagine life without her now and so far all is going wonderfully.

Lizzie was nearly 11 when she joined our family, which consisted of me and my then five-year-old birth daughter. Her history prior to coming to us was of early neglect and physical abuse, with multiple moves until the age of four, when she was placed for adoption. The adoption went through but broke down when she was nine, and whilst in foster care for just over a year she changed carers several times. Her previous adopters felt that she wasn't attached to them and that from the day she was placed she had tried to cause the breakdown that eventually occurred.

She was impulsive, aggressive, had no friends and was unable to sustain relationships, though she was superficially friendly with adults. At school she was destructive, disruptive and in a special unit 50 per cent of the time, with the rest of the day spent one-to-one. Her school would not have wished to continue long-term.

When Lizzie arrived I felt that I was well prepared and 'armed for battle'. I have had quite a lot of experience of children so I had strong ideas on how to do things. I didn't feel that this always went down too well with other involved parties, but in retrospect I think my ideas were valid. I received Lizzie with boxes and bags and the long-awaited information from previous carers. I found it a little alarming to read that she had attempted to strangle another child in her penultimate school and showed no sign of understanding the seriousness of what she had done. After all, I had a five-year-old. The timing of this news did make me laugh, but it was too late by then.

The slightly controversial ideas that I think have paid off are largely to do with my understanding of attachment. My goal was to get Lizzie communicating as opposed to reacting, to get her under control and to help her know what she was feeling and why. I believe that in the first instance a healthy attachment is created by the mother's presence, which provides security. A baby's world is wrapped up in its mother's, and the mother regulates the baby's world and makes it a safer place. I felt that until Lizzie had learned to attach I had to be available 100 per cent of the time. Hence my first obstacle. I wanted to be in school with her all day and every day. I wanted her to learn to let me deal with the situations she didn't have the resources to cope with – i.e. other people's jokes, a teacher's instruction that she didn't quite understand, and so on. I was concerned that if she spent seven hours a day away from me in a situation where all her life she had failed, any sort of relationship she might manage to build with me during the other hours would be cancelled out. I wanted her to come out of denial. We went to school together.

My next strategy was to allow her, at her request, to sleep in my bed. Once again, I was concerned to give her a safe world and wanted her to trust me. If she felt fear and I told her she must be good and sleep on her own, this would only teach her that she must squash her feelings.

During the early days I worked on the principle that Lizzie was not allowed further away from me than I could reasonably trust her. I did not make this a rule for her; it was a rule for me. This meant she was always in earshot. It was very demanding, but has paid off. I was very tough on disobedience and bad behaviour.

Lizzie is now one of the better-behaved children in her class. She no longer needs me to be in school with her all day, though I do give her three hours' academic help a week. This is so she can fulfil her potential. There are no outbursts at school and no acts of aggression. She never swears, and plays well with her sister. She has learned to play imaginatively and her co-ordination has improved no end. I feel she is attached to us.

I have been amazed at how much change there has been in such a short time. Lizzie also appreciates how different she is. We love her to bits!

Determined to make it work

The smile on Charlotte's face said it all. She had been successful in her GCSE exams, achieving eight high-grade passes, which meant that she would be able to do her chosen A levels and then go on to university if she so wished. She had worked hard for these exams and wanted to succeed in them. This has been the hallmark of her adoption with us.

Our first contact with Charlotte was through a photograph in the *Be My Parent* newspaper. The more we heard about Charlotte the more interested we were, and so we were thrilled when we were the family chosen by her social worker.

Charlotte moved into our family two months after her ninth birthday, six weeks after we first met her. Although she found it pretty strange to be living in a family with just one other child after having lived in a family where there had been two other girls to play with, plus at least two other foster children, she settled in fairly quickly. Of course, it was not easy for her or for us for the first few months as we all had a lot of adjusting to do.

Charlotte settled down well at her new school. School has always been an important part of her life, particularly in the early years when it provided her with structure and stability which was missing from her home life at the time.

Of course, things are not always hunky-dory, as everyone with teenagers in the family will know – but the problems we have had have been associated with age and not particularly with adoption.

Charlotte is a very happy, well-adjusted person who has loads of friends. She is very considerate and generous to a fault. Of course, she is not perfect – it is impossible for her to put anything away and consequently she is always losing things.

So what has made Charlotte's adoption work so well? A social worker from Barnardo's once said: 'It's a pity we can't bottle whatever it is that Charlotte has got and give some to our other children waiting for adoption.' I think that some factors contributing to this success have been a first-class adoption agency, excellent work done by Charlotte's social worker whilst she was in care, superb foster parents, who prepared her well for moving on, ongoing letter contact with the birth family, but most of all her own desire, either conscious or subconscious, to make the adoption work. As a Christian I have thanked God on numerous occasions for Charlotte, for giving us the opportunity to watch her grow into a happy, well-adjusted person, and for making our family complete.

CHAPTER 6

Adopting a Child with
a Physical or Learning Disability

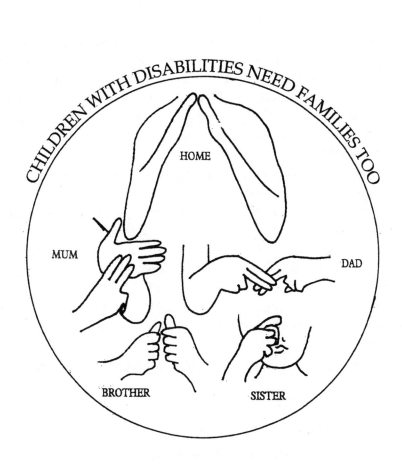

You can't do this on your own. Respite care, good educational facilities for your child's needs, and supportive medical and social care are essentials both for you and for the child you are adopting.

The physical wear and tear of looking after a child with special needs can exhaust the most adoring of parents if they don't stop for a few hours occasionally.

In adopting a child with a disability there are additional challenges. As well as having the insecurities, emotional needs, and individuality of character that makes each of us unique, these children have to deal with a body that won't work to order or a mind that leaves them behind as their peers move forward in life. 'It is one long battle to find everything from the right school to the right pair of shoes,' said one adopter.

These are the children who 25 years ago were considered 'unadoptable'. Since then, a number of agencies have been specially set up to find the unusual families that they need – families who are prepared to fight for children who can't fight for themselves. For them, adopting a disabled child is the right option, not a 'second choice', and brings just as much joy as the adoption of an able-bodied child. Many have an instinctive feeling that they can help one particular child, however severely disabled.

'We all have disabilities of some description – who and what is normal?' asks one successful adoptive mother.

An adopter of a child with Down's syndrome gives the following advice to others considering adopting a disabled child: 'Don't just discuss the idea, don't think "Oh, I couldn't" – you could!'

The delight for these adopters is in the happiness of their children and the physical progress they achieve, however small.

But the joy of adopting a child with a disability is often tinged with sadness, both as a result of the inabilities of the child and, sometimes, the shortness of their lives.

One adopter has drawn up a list of musts for parents of a child with a disability:

- accept life as it is
- laugh at situations when others might cry
- give until it hurts, even without response
- never give up, even if you seem to be getting nowhere
- put achievements before failures

- help him/her to accept himself/herself
- teach him/her to love. He/she must always be given a lot of love.

• • •

Mark and James

After endless discussions about what sort of child we could cope with, we concluded that they must not be above eight years old or mentally handicapped; anything else fine. With hope, we set off. Endless phone calls and letters came to no avail. Then the *Adoption UK Journal* came out. We planned to phone for details of the children of our choice the following day. The only child in the journal in our range was a three-and-a-half-year-old boy with Down's syndrome. Although we felt this was a handicap with which we couldn't cope, we decided to apply. The social worker wanted to meet us and we kept the appointment, thinking to ourselves, 'You never know, he may know of other children.' After long discussions we agreed to meet Mark, but we were pretty sure he wouldn't be coming to live with us.

We met Mark. We couldn't believe our emotions that day. We liked him and he appeared to like us. Perhaps the mental handicap wasn't as bad as we had thought. We returned a week later, and on this second meeting the fact that he was mentally handicapped had flown out of the window for us. We were too busy getting to know our son and making arrangements for him to come home.

The joys he has brought us are unbelievable. We have never regretted that decision to visit the little boy we didn't think we could cope with. Now we cannot imagine life without him! Each milestone he reaches brings us the greatest joy. The tears I shed before Mark arrived were of sorrow and sadness. Since his arrival the tears have been of laughter and pure joy. Two years later we saw James, who had a physical problem. We all took to him straight away. Now we have two loving, boisterous, mischievous little boys, which is more than I dared hope for at the beginning.

Surely we all have disabilities of some description! If my sons are disabled then I am the proudest disabled mum you are ever likely to meet. Yes, our boys have problems, one intellectual, the other physical; with both it is uncertain what they will achieve academically and physically. But I am confident in the knowledge that, with love and patience, our boys will grow to their full potential, no matter how great or small that may seem to others. To the four of us, every single achievement will be a wonderful thing.

Katie

We saw Katie's picture in a winter issue of the *Adoption UK Journal* when she was one year old. I had thought her too handicapped for our situation; my wife fell for her youth and blue eyes. We asked to hear more about her. Katie has thalidomide-type deformities, which include four shortened and twisted limbs, and many other problems with her eyes, ears, heart and internal organs.

We thought hard and then applied for her. After a lengthy assessment and visits to hospitals and special schools we were allowed to visit Katie at her Cheshire home. The staff there didn't want to part with her, and certainly not to an unconventional family which already contained three teenagers, a seven-year-old and a toddler. We, on our side, found that we didn't like Katie! Nothing to do with her disabilities, but she was fat, flabby, pale, lethargic and had straggly hair. Later, my wife spent several days getting to know her, and was told that Katie would need four hours' physiotherapy a day and major surgery within months. She liked her even less! But by now we had gone too far to draw back, so we duly took her home. (Now, of course, we love her dearly.)

She was bewildered and not too pleased with country life, but she and Maria (18 months old) took to each other at once and this close friendship enabled Katie to progress from sitting propped up to getting about in a baking tin at great speed. The older children would each take a baby under their arm when playing games about the farm.

On one of Katie's routine visits to the Limb Fitting Centre at Roehampton she was allowed to abandon her dangerous artificial legs and try out a Maldon go-kart, which was bought for her by a local businessman's club when she was three. This, we consider, was the biggest turning point in her life – she was free to go where she liked for the first time. Katie's deafness became an increasing handicap. It was only after years of tests, grommets, etc. that she was finally equipped with two large hearing aids, which wouldn't stay on her bat-like ears (she later had the ears adjusted). At five she went to full-time school for physically handicapped children.

Disturbed by Katie's lack of academic progress, we looked for a new school and for the first time encountered prejudice against her. Eventually we found the perfect school, a small primary 12 miles away. In spite of obstacles put in our way and gloomy prognostications, this adoption has been a great success. Katie is now an enthusiastic Brownie and attends Pony Club junior camp. She has recently had the long-threatened heart surgery. Katie is a happy child, sensible about her limitations but prepared to try anything. The problems we have had have not, on the whole, been those we were led to expect. There has been no revulsion from the public – on the contrary, she is very popular.

Philip

We have adopted two children, Philip and Jessica, both born with spina bifida. Philip has been in our care since he was 15 months old. We were told very little about him. After visiting him at a children's home for about an hour we were asked if we wanted to take him home. We would have but for the formality of some paperwork, and so we were told that we would have to come back again.

On our next visit we met his social worker, went straight out to Philip's foster home and spoke to his foster mother for about half an hour before we took him. She told us that he was quiet and that he ate mainly Guinness and chips. She spent most of her time telling us how having him had paid for her stair carpet!

Philip had been very badly treated and the way he was handed over was an indication of the lack of care and love that he had suffered. From birth he had been neglected by his parents, who were unable to care for him, and by all the authorities that had a responsibility to step in.

When we collected him he was covered in a nappy rash that extended nearly all over his body. He was overweight, and dribble and drink had caused sores around his mouth and neck. These were so bad that he looked as if he had been cut with a cheese wire. We were to discover that he had been kept in a cot or pram for most of his life, with nothing to do or look at. He just stared and showed no interest in anything or anybody. He made no effort to sit or crawl. He had not started to eat properly – with the exception of sucking chips. No teeth had come through. It was about a year before we broke through his emotional troubles and he began to learn to respond to our love.

We were always concerned that he was partially deaf and suffering from hydrocephalus, but were continually told that we were wrong and treated like neurotic parents who could not accept that their child was slow. When Philip was six we managed to 'con' the head surgeon at the Westminster Children's Hospital into looking at him. Within minutes, he was arranging for him to have a brain scan and proper hearing test. He was found to be severely brain-damaged due to uncorrected hydrocephalus – his brain was in fact only about one-sixth of the size it should have been – and a test at the Nuffield Centre showed that he was deaf in both ears. He could not hear high frequency sounds.

Plans were made to operate. The damage was done, but Philip has improved since the operations. He is brighter and can speak a little now.

Philip now attends a special school. He is very happy and gets on well with everybody. Although he is slow because of brain damage he is a very loving and kind child. Philip loves to help about the house or watch his dad working. He likes gardening or any activity in which he can use his hands.

The adoption of Jessica (who also has spina bifida) was in total contrast to Philip's. We had a slow introduction, we were told all about her and we were given a book of her life story. By the time we took her home she was very nearly one of the family.

Jessica has just started at an ordinary school. She is the only handicapped child there but she has had no problems settling down. She is a very extrovert and confident girl. She is determined and this is a great asset to her. Jessica is outgoing and loves to visit her friends up and down the road. She also likes music and dancing (Pink Floyd, Led Zeppelin and Thin Lizzy, as well as more simple tunes).

With our experience, we should now like to adopt another spina bifida child.

You can hold a conversation with someone who doesn't talk

David is quadriplegic: he can only move his head and needs total care. The only person to really try to stop his adoption was his paediatrician, who was concerned that ordinary people couldn't look after someone so disabled as David.

When David first came he screamed all night and also screamed if he couldn't make us understand what he wanted or if we weren't doing things quickly enough. He once screamed for three hours solid at a very posh wedding we went to.

We have had to learn to ignore people staring at us, and remarks made to us such as, 'You must get paid well,' or, 'Children like him should be in a home,' and so on. We have learnt who our real friends are.

Having three teenagers in the house is great fun! Of the eight children born to us, only Iain and Anna remain at home. Iain and Anna have been very good with David. Having him with us has been a big change in their lives.

In his own way, David has taught people that they can hold a conversation with someone who doesn't talk and that he doesn't choke too easily if they feed him. He has a wicked sense of humour and is very aware of what is going on around him. He goes to a very good school and is learning to communicate through computers using rebus symbols. Things are getting easier; this year's holiday was much better than last year's. Most of his problems were the result of living in a home. After two years he has put on weight and seems to have matured. But it is still very hard to know what age he is at – sometimes he is like a small child, whereas sometimes he is like a stroppy teenager.

With a child like David, if you follow your own instincts and stand by them – sometimes against the experts' advice – you can generally overcome problems. For instance, we felt that David wouldn't want a room of his own; he loves to share with Iain. David was cuddled like a small child when the nights were at their worst. Above all, David likes to be treated as much like the other children in our family as possible. We have done lots of things the wrong way round. We have learnt to decorate a room with a child watching every move from a large wheelchair. David has had to learn that it's not funny when someone hurts themselves, that the same people who are up all night are also up all day, and that if you don't like someone they don't go off shift.

We don't know what the future holds for David, but we do know he will always be loved and cared for by his family. All our lives have been so enriched by David being part of our family, and we are so pleased that he loves being one of us.

Michael (real name)

During the night of 22 November my adopted son Michael died peacefully in his sleep. He was just three years old.

Michael and I first met each other just over two years previously, after a long search that ended in a residential children's home in London. There I saw a very small, beautiful baby boy. Staff and social workers were anxiously watching our reactions to each other; would I, an inexperienced single woman, be able to cope with this totally dependent child with severe cerebral palsy and chronic breathing problems, and would Michael be able to adapt to living in a family home, when all he had been used to was the regime of a nursery, with a different carer every day?

We both decided there and then that we loved each other, and after an exhausting introductory week in which I had endless meetings with doctors, therapists, etc., my mother came to take us home. And therein lies another story. My mother had been very much against the idea of me adopting a handicapped child, yet here she was picking up this little scrap and exclaiming, 'But he is lovely!' And so started a mutual love affair.

Michael found some aspects of home life very strange. On the first day home, desperate to show off my beautiful baby, I strapped him into a brand new pushchair and set off to do the shopping. Screams and sobs from the pushchair, which after 15 minutes I could no longer ignore, forced us to return home rapidly. When the social workers visited the following week I learnt that Michael had never been outside except in a car! He took some time to get used to walks, but he revelled in other aspects of home life and made deep attachments to his new extended family.

We had two very happy years together, and for the first year he remained fairly healthy. But the second year saw the start of asthma attacks and a series of hospital admissions. Despite this, Michael led a very full social life. He went swimming and riding, joined a music group, had holidays abroad, and attended a small nursery school for two terms. This was a nursery school where the staff had not previously had a handicapped child, and yet the two afternoons a week that Michael spent there were probably his happiest hours; here was a severely disabled child, who couldn't move or speak, joining in with a class of two to three-year-olds and loving every minute of it.

On the night of 22 November I put my little boy to bed. He had been a little off colour during the day, but nothing to prepare me for the shock of finding him dead the next morning.

Of course, the inevitable questioning began. Was I right in letting Michael go to nursery school and taking him swimming and riding, thus exposing him to too many infections? Should I have kept him at home? But neither of us would have enjoyed this kind of existence and many letters I received after his death remarked on how much he had enjoyed his short life. One mother whose son attended the nursery group wrote that her little boy had asked repeatedly to have Michael come home to play with him. On the day before he died, she had asked the teacher which child Michael was and whether he be able to come and play; she didn't even know that he was handicapped. The inscription on the beautiful flowers they sent to the funeral read: 'To Michael, my first school friend.'

Michael had a dramatic effect on all the people who met him and I believe this was his purpose in life. In spite of his short time on this earth he probably changed the attitudes of over 100 people towards the handicapped.

Natalie (real name)

I'm a mature mum with a grown-up family, a daughter of 24 and sons of 22 and 19, and last year we were joined by Natalie, who is now nearly four. I adopted Natalie through Parents for Children. Step by step I was told what life would be like with her, but nobody consulted Natalie and she changed the rules on placement overnight.

Before she arrived I had long talks with my placement worker. Things I identified as of possible benefit included special-needs schooling, a child development clinic, a physiotherapist, a hydrotherapy pool, and Riding for the

Disabled, to name but a few. We discussed everything from schooling, my children, finance, respite care, the past and the future.

I was told many times that Natalie was severely mentally and physically disabled. She screamed and screamed for long periods and was generally unmanageable – but in my heart I didn't believe it. I had seen the video of Natalie and it just did not fit.

I was taken to see various people connected with Natalie, including her paediatrician and physiotherapist, but the most helpful and positive person was her respite carer. The foster parents were not certain that a single mum would be able to cope.

By the time placement came I thought I knew everything about Natalie. I had spent four days and one night with the foster family before placement and will admit that I nearly backed out when the foster mother said Natalie would 'ruin my life'. For one tired moment I wanted to run.

I am glad I didn't. Natalie is an absolute joy. She is severely athetoid and has cerebral palsy but is mentally bright. She is able to use her home computer (bought with money raised by local folk), knows 20 Makaton symbols so far, and eye-points or moves her arm and hand laboriously to touch the symbol she is indicating, i.e. her sister, or food, or the car – although never her potty!

I was well prepared by Parents for Children; I was given all the information they had about Natalie. What they didn't know I soon discovered for myself. Natalie's eyesight is not what it should be; and earlier in the summer she had grommets fitted for very severe glue ear. The ENT (ear, nose and throat) specialist said the noises in her head would have been unbearable at times – remember the screaming?

She was also dreadfully constipated and came to me with a bottle of lactulose and instructions on manual extraction of faeces. Now that she is on a diet of fresh vegetables, fish but no meat, rice puddings, bananas and at least a pint of milk a day she is no longer constipated and is growing rapidly and putting on weight.

I sometimes feel angry that Natalie was labelled a screamer without anyone wondering whether there were any underlying problems. Where was the health visitor? Why didn't Natalie have the usual eye checks and hearing tests? Why give her lactulose for constipation without attempting to sort out her diet? Natalie suffered needlessly for much of the first two and a half years of her life.

At the time of placement I believed I knew what I was taking on, but Natalie changed the rules and became a darling little girl. Had she stayed 'difficult'. I was prepared – whether I would have stayed sane is another matter!

Christopher

We first met Christopher last July, and a month later he came home to live with us. We hadn't specifically set out to adopt a child with Down's syndrome, but we had always said we would consider a child with a disability. Christopher was nine months old when we first saw him, with a smile that could melt the coldest heart. Now he is almost one year older, and still has that smile.

The past year has seen our lives turned upside down. From being set in our childless ways we have become a real family. Christopher has brought true joy into our lives and indeed the lives of all he meets, from his music group leader, who has never seen such enthusiasm in anyone for playing the bells, to a besotted grandad.

All our fears have been unfounded – they were really just fears of the unknown. We have had tremendous support both through the official channels and from friends and family. There are many facilities available for 'special' children like Christopher, but his most important need is for a mum and dad to be a family with.

Having Christopher has made us look at life with new eyes. He will never enjoy those things that society traditionally regards as important – academic achievement, brilliant career, financial success – but he is the happiest person I know in the true sense of the word and will always be very special to us in so many ways.

Adam

Adam suffers from cerebral palsy and is diaplegic. When we first went to see him he was 18 months old, had been in a number of foster homes, and was not a pretty sight. He was fat and awkward and spent most of the time shuffling around the floor on his back. However, we felt he had enormous potential, and after visiting him a number of times to establish a relationship we began to foster Adam. We adopted him when he was three.

After Adam arrived we soon realised that doctors and social workers do not always agree with each other. Some saw Adam as little more than a cabbage, whereas others saw a child who could have a bright future. Happily, the latter were correct. Over the years he has made tremendous progress. He is able now to attend normal school, leads a happy life, and has lots of outside interests.

Our experience is that would-be adopters of handicapped children need plenty of determination. Look for the potential in a child and then realise that through hard work – yours and theirs – that potential can be realised. If you are persuaded that the child is right for you, then don't let well-intentioned relatives, friends or professionals put you off. Do ask around for help and advice. We found that we did have to ask. Our experience has been that hard work and determination have paid dividends.

Once a bruvver, always a bruvver

To the social workers he was a multi-jeopardised, stateless ethnic minority refugee with a learning disability, adopted by a racially naive white family. To the nasty bullies on the bridge who taunted him he was ching-chong-Chinaman-yellow-skin-slitty-eyes-no-brain. To my parents' former friends he was odd, possibly unsanitary and certainly daft.

To me, he is my bruvver.

He is absolutely my bruvver.

There was only ever one moment when I doubted whether he should have become part of our family. He'd been living with us for about a year. I was desperate to ask my mother a question about my homework but my brother was in a particularly demanding mood, kicking the table and rocking from side to side. It required all our mother's energy to keep him engaged with a story book. She couldn't break off from devoting her attention to him without running the risk of him getting furious or sulky. In my instant irritation at him for monopolising my mother I suddenly saw him as others did. I could hear the questions asked of me by those curious friends of my parents.

'Do you mind having a disabled brother?'

'Do you actually like him?'

'It must be frightfully difficult for you normal children.'

And I understood the ignorance and hostility behind them.

Apart from that disloyal moment he has always been a brother. He does all the things most brothers do. Sometimes he needs looking after, like when he got the shingles when our parents were on holiday. Sometimes he needs affection, like when he is remembering that he was handed into an orphanage and wondering about his first parents, of whom he knows nothing. Sometimes he looks after me, like when I was very depressed and he would suddenly hug me and say, 'I hope you be better soon.'

Sometimes he does brilliant jokes, like on New Year's Eve in a country pub after hours, when all the villagers were dancing to the jukebox and one of our brother's favourite rock tracks came on. Having been ambling back from the toilet doing up his flies he suddenly recognised the tune and flung himself into a knee skid, coming to a halt in the middle of the brick floor. He then performed an air guitar solo, to the amazement of other drinkers and the delighted hilarity of his siblings.

His turns of phrase have passed into our family's collective vocabulary, like 'Splash you!' when someone has sneezed instead of the more usual, 'Bless you!'

His difficulties with reading or counting are the least important things in a description of what sort of a person he is, but to many caregivers what they call a 'learning disability' is his defining feature. As I see it, he doesn't have a problem learning things, it's just that he forgets them again immediately. The discomfort that our society feels when dealing with slow people shows in what they're called. There are so many convoluted terms, which we use in order to distance ourselves from the moral judgements and overtones associated with calling someone 'stupid'. People who can't write, talk, count or think very well are assumed to be morally or emotionally inferior to those who are literate, articulate, numerate and quick thinking. And as fast as new terms are invented, old connotations catch up, rendering the new words insulting as well.

People like my bruv don't need any new phrases to describe the things which make their lives difficult. He and we need sufficient support so that we can all get on with the discovery of our abilities and pleasures in family life.

Being Jack's mum

On a day that brought to a head nearly a week of difficult days, on which Jack, a child with special needs, and I had been really quite cross with and horrible to one another – a combination of hormones (me), worry (me), teething and coughing (Jack), and lack of sleep (both of us) – I sat down in the evening to write down a few things and try to work out what was going wrong. I was having doubts in my ability to parent and thinking that it was all my fault that things were going badly. I didn't feel like a very kind mummy at all. This was a time when I really felt that single parenthood was hard. However, writing helped me to sort it out and made the days that followed much easier, because I was ready to be a mum again.

I don't like…no, to be honest, I hate…Jack clinging on to me *all day*, whining and wiping his snotty nose all over me.

…the never-ending battle over food: I'm tired of mashing, blending and stirring all manner of nourishing food – high fat, high protein and carefully balanced with capsules of pancreatic enzyme – only to have it end up in the bin, rejected.

…the wrestling match of getting clothes on and off, all those layers. And then, as the final zip on the snow suit goes up, the ghastly smell of yet another nappyful rising to meet me.

…the fact that Jack seems to know how to wind me up, repeatedly going back to the same forbidden things.

...the fact that I can't go to my evening class tonight because the babysitter can't come after all.

I love...the sound of him babbling over the baby alarm in the morning;

...his earnest attempts to watch lips and imitate speech;

...his smile...his giggle...his whole body laughing so hard he falls over;

...his face, his expressions;

...his dancing;

...his pride in himself when he knows he's done something clever;

...his face and eyebrows and tongue when he's concentrating hard;

...his awe and wonderment at this beautiful world;

...his hair, gleaming in the sunshine;

...his little, vulnerable flower stem of a neck;

...his appearance from behind in a pair of dungarees;

...his little flat feet;

...his skin, so soft, so warm;

...the smell of him fresh from the bath;

...the warmth of him cuddled in my arms;

...his neediness, sad and sick, drooping on my shoulder;

...that he looks for me and runs to me;

...that he calls me 'Ah-Mama'...

CHAPTER 7

Adopting an Emotionally, Physically or Sexually Abused Child

These are the children for whom your nightmares have been a reality. The horror of what has happened to them will probably haunt them in some way for the rest of their lives, however much care and love adoptive parents or foster carers give them.

They have been the innocent victims of evil behaviour. Their past is often so deeply buried in their subconsciouses that they don't understand why certain everyday events, sounds and words can trigger panic and make them shiver with fear. One foster mother of a sexually abused child recounted how her foster child screamed every time she turned on the Hoover.

Though desperately in need of understanding and appropriate love and care, abused children often find it hard to accept such care and respond appropriately to it. Those who were supposed to love them most and teach them how to love were also those who abused them.

'Caring for children who have been sexually abused can be a daunting task for the most committed carer. Because of the horrendous previous experiences of some of these children their behaviour can be so extreme that placements disrupt at a most alarming rate,' says the director of a residential project caring for grossly sexually abused children.

She believes that in order to stop a breakdown a high therapeutic input is needed both before and after a child is placed. 'The healing process for a sexually abused child is likely to take a lifetime. The carer needs to be helped to obtain the skills to help the child.'

All such children need very careful handling. The rules of the house must be clear: an old-fashioned bear-hug from dad is probably off the agenda almost permanently. 'They have to be shown how to love appropriately and to understand what love is,' said one seasoned adopter.

But many adopters of emotionally, sexually or physically abused children take them on without anyone realising the depths of what they have been through.

'It is like a time bomb waiting to go off. And at an unlikely moment, perhaps when a child is suddenly feeling secure at last, the horrifying truth of their past comes tumbling out,' said another adopter.

Unprepared, the adoptive family may not know where to turn or what to do next to help their son or daughter to cope with this nightmare. Despite widespread acceptance of the problems of physically and sexually abused children, help is often scarce and inadequate – their problems are easy for society to ignore or blame on hyperactivity, adolescence, stupidity and a bundle of other common problems rather than the horrifying truth.

Even once accepted there is no universal remedy for their problems. Some need to regress to their earliest childhood days; others don't. A combination of personal traits and circumstances makes each child unique in his or her ability to cope and to come to terms with the past.

The most difficult challenge for many adopters is that they don't just have to fight for help for their child but also for help for themselves to deal with and handle their child's behaviour. But, as one adopter said of a physically abused child: 'Conventional wisdom cannot always be trusted. Parents' own judgement and knowledge of their child, adopted or not, is often the most reliable guide.'

Adopters of abused children need a double dose of emotional strength and determination. But the rewards of helping a child through the nightmare are enormous. An adopter of a sexually abused child who was 'frozen' (she flinched if anyone touched her and touched no one) remembers what for her was the final breakthrough – three years after adoption. 'Something had really upset me and I was standing in the kitchen shedding a few tears. Diana came up to me, quite spontaneously put her arms around me and *she* gave *me* a cuddle. I knew then that we would win.'

• • •

Post-trauma syndrome

Our daughter came to live with us 12 years ago. She had been consistently and brutally physically abused throughout the first year of her life to the point where she was not expected to live.

Our daughter is happy as a member of our family and progresses well in most ways. There are, however, some permanent problems which she came with and which do not change year after year. We have finally sought psychiatric advice and the diagnosis is post-trauma syndrome.

The psychiatrist explained that victims can be walking down a street and suddenly have a severe anxiety attack triggered by something they see, but not understand what is happening.

The symptoms which our daughter shows are clear and persistent. They all relate to a deep fear, in her case of experiences so early that she cannot remember them. The symptoms appear unrelated until you realise they can all be explained by fear of attack. She faints at the most trivial injury; for instance, a tiny scratch or a broken fingernail. She has tremendous problems forming close relationships with her peer group. She cannot tolerate any aggression from them such as teasing or arguments, and withdraws, which makes it impossible for her to have normal teenage relationships. She is over-organised and conscientious around any authority figure. I instinctively treat her very lightly in terms of control or discipline because I have always sensed that she is frightened of me. These symptoms can apparently be explained by the fact that she is living with fear all the time.

The rage of an abused child

My understanding is that physically abused children feel let down by adults and are full of blistering rage against all adults and often the world in general. They have lost all trust in relationships, parental or otherwise, so they constantly test adults, particularly parents, with unruly behaviour coupled with moral and emotional blackmail. So entrenched are they in these habitual, morose and negative patterns of behaviour that they are unable to think or reason and can only react to how a situation feels at any given moment. This leaves them unable to learn from previous similar experiences and apply that knowledge to the current situation.

At the moment my wife and I are totally frustrated and angry at having to go round and round in ever-decreasing circles. Our daughter hates school, hates herself and believes she is unloved. Bizarre behaviour, such as hiding dirty and often soiled clothing under the bed and in drawers together with rotten sandwiches and empty sweet and crisp packets, is never-ending.

The relationship between my wife and daughter is extremely fraught. My wife bends over backwards to try to accommodate our daughter only to have everything thrown back in her face. When she is in a good frame of mind, our daughter is all over my wife, constantly wanting to do things with her and not giving her a minute's peace. Our daughter's behaviour is false, and it is suffocating that my wife has to be on her best behaviour, knowing that any wrong comment or inflection of voice will incur a violent reaction of temper followed by days of sullen hatred. It is virtually a love-hate relationship.

This makes our daughter impossible to live with to such a degree that when she goes to her respite foster carer to stay for occasional weekends we are both glad to see her go so that we can have space to ourselves.

It is quite obvious that the counselling given by the clinical psychologist to our daughter is having no effect whatsoever. We have constantly stated this to our counsellor and all we get is: 'Your daughter is a severely damaged child and there are no absolute guarantees. However, she is in touch with the negative parts of her trauma and is being helped to address them.' These professionals will not give us the proper written assessment that we have asked for constantly.

I feel our daughter needs in-depth hypnotherapy or psychotherapy to gradually get to the heart of the problem. I believe that in her case counselling, however well delivered, is like trying to cure cancer with aspirin. I don't believe it can get through the natural subconscious defence mechanisms that she has built up through (I suspect) slyness, deliberate lies and pretending there is nothing wrong. This leaves her totally unable to mature, either emotionally or educationally. A pretty bleak future, I have to admit.

Different ages, different child

Children who have been severely neglected have so many facets to their experiences, personalities and behaviour that at times, as a parent, you begin to wonder whether or not you've gone mad. How can this child, who just ten minutes ago was playing cricket in the park, now be curled up on the bed saying, 'Mummy, I want a bottle'?

We know very little of our children's early lives other than that they were severely neglected. At his three-year-old check Ben was asked by the health visitor to do something with a doll. He didn't know what the doll was for and his grandmother said he'd never seen one before. We are aware that there were few if any toys and no television in their home and that for a long period prior to coming into care the boys hadn't been out of the flat. As we got to know them we began to realise that they hadn't had soft toys to go to sleep with and therefore didn't express a need for them. Even though they both were given teddies on their arrival, and picked up other soft toys, it wasn't until six months into placement that we noticed they actually wanted their toy animals in bed with them.

From seeing baths as quick in-and-out affairs they began to play with boats, turtles and other toys in the bath.

When Ben first came to us he couldn't play with toys. Eventually, after about four months, he started playing with the Playmobile garage and making up stories. Just recently he has started playing make-believe with other children but tends to avoid it if there is a distraction such as a bike or a football.

We found that both children needed to play with the 'early' toys – simple jigsaws, musical instruments, sorting boxes – before they could play with toys more appropriate for their age. They had no concept of numbers, so we spent every night without fail playing games for 15 minutes before bed, starting off with snap, lotto, ludo and listening games. Although it drove us mad with boredom sometimes, we realised that it was important because the children were learning numbers, how to take turns and how to lose.

Play is such an important part of a child's life that Ben's and Alex's inability to play made them stand out as different more than the fact that they were so far behind educationally (Ben was three and a half years behind, Alex one and a half years). It's been really important for them to learn to relax at the park, to know that they don't need to tear around and do everything at once because the park and the opportunity to go to the park will be there another day.

The lack of ability to play affects children's social development. It meant that although Ben and Alex could keep up with others playing football or cycling, they didn't have the make-believe – the sense of what to do with Lego or how to play with cars – that is a way in to playing with others.

One of the hardest areas to understand has been their emotional development. By emotions I mean the ability to say how you feel, to recognise feelings and to be aware of yourself and your effect on others. When they first came, Ben and Alex found it very hard to show their feelings other than through their behaviour. Ben would break a toy if it didn't work properly or do what he wanted it to do. He would hit us if told off or swear to get attention. He very rarely cried nor did he like to sit and be cuddled. Alex was afraid to receive hugs and would go off by himself if upset rather than let someone else comfort him. Each of the boys regressed into nappies and using baby bottles at their own request.

Gradually, as we talked with them, we began to give them the vocabulary they needed to tell us their feelings. We would ask questions such as, 'Do you feel angry? Sometimes I have a big ball of anger in me and I need someone to listen to me to help it get out,' or, 'Are you excited? You look excited.' They are beginning to tell us more how they feel. It's exciting when they say, 'I need a cuddle.'

Another area they've found difficult is recognising the effect their behaviour has on others. When you've lived with people who have ignored you, you want their attention but you don't necessarily understand what other people need from you. So we are trying to help them learn this through saying things to them such as: 'That makes me feel happy, thank you. You showed you cared by getting me a glass of water.'

One of the hardest things is that parenting children who have so many facets to their personalities means I often make mistakes in my interactions with them. Sometimes I tell off the eight-year-old Ben in the way you speak to eight-year-olds, but as his understanding of my argument is at a five-year-old level he doesn't follow all my points and so reacts emotionally like a three-year-old.

The longer the children have been with us the more they have caught up, but I know it will be many years before we will really be able to see them as they are, fulfilling their potential and feeling secure enough to be relaxed and happy. They might always have difficulty at school but the most important thing is that they learn to be able to be with other people and to give and receive love.

Update 1999: We've now got two good-looking younger teenagers. At 14 and 12 they are both at mainstream school. They have both represented our local borough at sport and have a wide range of hobbies such as sailing, golf, canoeing, war gaming, bell-ringing and Scouts. They have a wide network of friends.

Many children regress – aggression in adolescence in not uncommon, so what is the difference for adopters? The difference for us is that our children often regress to an age at which we were not their parents, when no one was meeting their emotional needs. Friends of mine will say, 'Sarah [15] is being really difficult. She's behaving just as she did when she started school – just because she is nervous.' I wasn't there when my boys were five. When they were five the things that were paramount to them were feeling unsafe, being abused and moving families, so when they regress their behaviour can reflect the chaotic, out-of-control existence they had at that age.

Seven years as a family and many good times together have helped us to bond – we are proud of the boys and of what they have achieved. We realise that the times when they regress are further apart and that when they recover they move forward again.

As we move forward with the boys, we celebrate their lives and their courage and know we've changed through loving them.

An educative experience

Our son was placed for adoption at the age of five after having been in care for over two years. My husband and I adopted him four months later and he has now been with us for five years.

Emotional and/or physical abuse of our son was suspected. During our assessment we were invited to consider possible difficulties we might face in bringing him up. We believed we were unshockable and prepared for anything. But nothing could have prepared us for the intense prejudice he encountered, especially from teachers and others in education authorities.

Our son was expected to present difficult behaviour. At school he had been disruptive and violent. Staff had been kicked, hit and bitten. They reported temper tantrums, attention-seeking behaviour and hyperactivity. Our son was 'unable' to learn because of his emotional state, which was explained as his reaction to emotional rejection. He was treated like a three-year-old. Teachers claimed he had regressed.

We were told to expect testing-out behaviour and that our son would 'see how far he could go' before we rejected him. But most of this advice was wrong. Bonding with him was easy: he was a loving child who wanted to be loved. Bright and talented, he asked for dancing classes and violin lessons. He now also plays piano and trumpet.

With strongly held views of his own, he required firm discipline, but never presented behaviour beyond our control. School was different. There were reports of aggressive violence and disturbed behaviour. All the Local Education Authority staff assumed he was 'emotionally disturbed' because of his life history. None suggested alternative explanations. Eventually, he was excluded from school and an LEA psychologist, who never saw him, recommended placement in a school for children with emotional and behavioural difficulties (EBD). Thus began a three-year battle to prove our son was not disturbed. The EBD school was devastating for our son. We removed him after three weeks, fearing for his psychological and physical safety (two years later, child protection teams investigated allegations of abuse by staff at this school).

Our son was excluded from three other primary schools for aggressive, violent and disruptive behaviour. We constantly clashed with teachers who, while demanding our co-operation, never listened to our advice or heeded our son's protests at their treatment of him. They treated our son as a child of half his age. Teachers and ancillaries who made him look ridiculous to his peers complained about his poor social skills. Our son's distress was attributed to parental incompetence.

A year after he had first been excluded from school we obtained independent assessments of our son. They showed that he had specific learning difficulties – dyslexia and a related orthoptic difficulty that impaired his reading also. This was treated and rectified within six months.

Presented with this information, LEA staff reluctantly acknowledged their misdiagnosis. Officers authorised payment of fees for an independent school with special tuition. After four terms he returned to a local school. With some additional support our son is now able to work successfully alongside his peers. He has age-appropriate treatment. His disturbed behaviour has ceased.

My husband is a consultant clinical psychologist. Well-educated professionals, we managed to resist intense pressure to accept the misdiagnosis of our son's difficulties. Our son was not recognised as a typical bright, extroverted dyslexic because of preconceptions about adopted children. With hindsight, all our son's behaviour, from the time he started school, can be explained as the consequence of this learning difficulty. He was denied the help he could and should have been given for three years. Consequently, he lacks confidence in his ability to succeed academically and is still underachieving in this area. The moral of this story is that while adopters are told to expect emotional problems, problems that appear to be emotional may have entirely different causes. Conventional wisdom cannot always be trusted. Parents' own judgement and knowledge of their child, adopted or otherwise, is often the most reliable guide.

The ingredients of success

Ours is a happy tale! At the beginning was a sense of relief when the gynaecologist told me that there was absolutely no hope of my having my own children. After all, this was something I had suspected for years. Adoption was a subject that was often discussed by members of my extended family, and so we wasted no time in getting to grips with it.

Once we were approved for adoption we settled down for a long wait. Three weeks later the phone rang. Our social worker from Childlink described a child, a wilful but healthy three-year-old. Her birth parents' background had a lot of similarities with ours. We did not need a lot of time to think about it, and gratefully said yes.

We were like children unable to wait until Christmas Day before opening their presents!

I also started to worry. Would I be a good parent? Would I be able to deal appropriately with situations as they arose? A friend of mine gave me some sound advice: 'You can only try, after all you are human. The most important thing is to get the message across to the child that you love her and always will.'

Our attachment to her grew after she moved in with us. As for now, it is impossible for us to imagine our lives without her. It is impossible for us to envisage loving any other child as much as we do her. We are also very content about her attachment to us.

Early in the placement we found out that our daughter had a chronic sleeping problem. I spent a lot of time thinking about what could have caused it, when it had started, and so on. Those were difficult times. I was up half of the night with her, trying everything I could think of to relax her (massage, soft music, oil burners, etc.). I was exhausted during the day, desperately trying to cope with a ratty, angry, tired child.

I started to sleep on the floor of our daughter's room. She was reassured to find me when she awoke and I got good sleep and was able to cope better with her during the day.

The other problem that we discovered nearly two months into the placement was frantic and compulsive masturbation. We informed the local authority at a review meeting shortly after.

Looking back at that review meeting, I do not think they gave any weight to our suspicion that our daughter might have practised mutual masturbation with another child at the foster home. The foster mum was 'unable' to help us on this matter either. Actually, the information that our daughter eventually volunteered led us to believe that what had happened in the foster home was bordering on sexual abuse.

When we first found out about it, we spent many sleepless nights wondering what had really happened to her. We decided to deal with the situation in a positive manner, i.e. to deal with the problem and protect the child in a way that minimised the long-term effects without alarming the child and provoking any feelings of shame or guilt. If she chooses to tell us more, she will in her own time. This has, so far, proved to be the right course of action.

I would like to summarise what, in our opinion, was the recipe for our success:

1. Excellent support from our social worker, who did a lot of listening.

2. Support from another adoptive parent with whom we became good friends.

3. I have used homeopathy for the last six years for myself and have faith in its effectiveness. We used it for our daughter initially to ease the pain of the move and help her deal with her anger, grief and feelings of abandonment. I believe it has helped a great deal with the forming of a sound attachment. We also used it effectively to deal with the sleeplessness and masturbation.

4. Support from family and friends who were rejoicing in our achievements.

5. Last but not least (we think it was quite important in our daughter's case), that we adapted the way we apply our rules and principles of child upbringing to suit her personality.

Living with a hurt child

We so often forget that the results of early trauma, neglect and abuse affect our adopted children's lives constantly. Both my son and daughter had suffered and still do suffer the effects of gross neglect, abuse for them being secondary. Sadly, the social, medical and educational services have allowed them to retreat from reality; my daughter, for instance, has been placed in a pupil referral unit with practically one-to-one teaching and excused daily for her unusual behaviours rather than having them dealt with.

We can give these children the world and more, but we can never compensate for the early losses they have suffered. All we can do is support them, and model good attachment, which is fundamental. We have to remember, too, that children cannot wait five to ten years to recover – so we, and our social work professionals and educators, do them no favours by pussyfooting around.

As a parent I am continually angered when I hear social workers say that if children don't want help we can't make them accept it: as though these poor youngsters know what's good for them! My two don't know what they want today, let alone tomorrow!

Unfortunately, we had incredibly inaccurate information about both our adopted children; correct information could have helped us avoid some major issues. Our second child came with little past history, and we were only able to get more information four years after her adoption.

Social work training without specialist knowledge of adoption and attachment is useless. We need effective resources, especially in therapy.

The family is still proven to be the best place for these children. Let's help one another and work together more. Maybe we can ease the unnecessary pain and isolation we have been left with after adopting our sad and traumatised children.

The boy with the short fuse

The day little Tommy completed our large family was the day things changed for ever.

Never again could we listen to music without hearing the beat tapped out on chairs, tables, saucepans or whatever he could find. Never again could we enjoy gospel choir music without hearing the entire choir echoed back, one harmony after another. Never again could we tap our feet gently to the music without little Tommy leaping around and dancing the best steps we've ever seen.

Take Michael Jackson as a little boy. Add a healthy dose of blues from Ray Charles, reggae from Shaka Demas and drumming from Phil Collins and you have some idea of the little boy who joined us.

Over the years Tommy has had to prove his worth by being the best in the house at building with Lego and the most artistic and cleverest in his school at history, science and wars. At the age of 11 he even won a prestigious school literary prize.

Our lives changed in other ways too. Tommy, whose first 16 months of life had been fraught with anxiety, made worse by his psychotic mother, made a beeline for his new mummy and formed a bond stronger than superglue. No one else was allowed a look in.

Tommy became an expert at controlling and manipulating the rest of the family. He learnt how to twist his oldest brother around his little finger. The two became locked in a mortal combat that continues to this day. He blamed others for bad behaviour such as his swearing, lying and stealing. He developed obsessions with fire, water, guns, knives and war.

When Tommy reached the age of three we hoped he would soon grow out of the 'terrible twos' stage of development. By the time he was nine we were still waiting, and realised that we had a bit of a challenge on our hands. We decided to seek help.

Outside the home Tommy has become a risk to himself and others. He walks impulsively across roads without looking. He goes out of his way to challenge and pick fights with other children.

At school he swears at teachers, walks out when he is told off and tries to hurt adults he doesn't like.

At home he causes daily chaos. Sometimes we wonder how long it will be before we can no longer cope. We need help: special-needs support at school, respite care, financial help and expert help.

It's not an easy task raising an adopted child like Tommy. Many people have wondered why we didn't give up years ago. Our answer is that after ten years Tommy is a vital part of our family, even if he is like a bomb with a short fuse.

We are angry that Tommy was so damaged emotionally in his first few months of life, and we are turning that anger into a fight for help and support. If we can win this battle it could set a precedent for hundreds of other adoptive families who face daily the terror of the short fuse.

Diana

When Diana came to us she was 13. A six-year placement had ended with a lot of pain, and I knew that I had to help her work through this pain but felt there was something else hidden to search out. She was a 'frozen' child. She could not bear to be touched and her feelings were so deeply hidden that she had very few normal reactions and did nothing spontaneously.

Six weeks later I learned from her social worker that at the age of four she had been sexually abused by her stepfather. This was the key. The sexual abuse had to be dealt with. But how, when she could not acknowledge it and probably had no conscious memory of it?

I started working to help her accept my touches. I set myself a daily task of touching her in a non-threatening way six times. I would brush imaginary hairs from her sleeve; imaginary wrinkles in her sweater would be smoothed; I would take her hand to feel how cold mine was; I would stroke her hair as I told her she had pretty highlights in it. At first she went rigid at my touch, but very gradually she relaxed and after many months I could cuddle her.

I started some direct work to put her in touch with her feelings and to try to help her remember what it was like to be four years old. The breakthrough came when we were playing with wooden building blocks. She embarked on a fantastic building. When it was nearly finished, I role-played the naughty child and demolished it. She was so angry, her eyes filled with tears; she was a four-year-old again.

That evening she came downstairs and asked if we could talk. It all came spilling out: her memories of her stepfather, his violence, the overwhelming unclean feeling when she thought about him. Other memories tumbled out. 'I think I must have been abused by him,' she said. That was the first of many talks on the subjects of abuse, bad dreams, sex and, later on, loving relationships.

At 15 we set out to find a suitable therapist for her. I had felt very pleased to be able to hand these problems over to a specialist in the field. She had finally acknowledged the abuse, her feelings about it and that she needed specialist help. And we had built up a special relationship that would still be with us while she was having therapy sessions.

Just before she was 16 a nice thing happened. Something had really upset me and I was standing in the kitchen shedding a few tears. Diana came up to me, quite spontaneously put her arms around me and *she* gave *me* a cuddle. I knew then that we would win.

CHAPTER 8

Unusual Adopters for Unusual Children

Single Parents, Unmarried and Gay Couples, and Adoption over Birth by Choice

Cadwgan Thomas

There is no such thing as a perfect family. However hard adoption agencies try to find them for the children in their care, not one of us is faultless.

But unconventional families – single adopters and unmarried and gay couples – are often considered too great a risk for an agency to take on, despite the number of children in care in need of a different kind of home than that offered by a conventional couple.

One single male social worker who after making more than 30 applications finally adopted a 12-year-old boy says: 'I know that in my own local authority there are numerous "difficult" children requiring placements, and yet we still turn down people who could be viable carers. We still seek the sort of perfection sought in applicants for healthy babies, where the supply-and-demand equation is very different.

'The reality is that there are not hoards of ordinary conventional families queueing up to foster or adopt our most damaged children. Besides, many such youngsters could not survive in such placements – some have already experienced several disruptions. Children get condemned to remain in residential care (which itself can be damaging) because they are labelled "unfosterable" – a label that often relates not to the behaviour of the child but to the narrowness of placement options available.

'What is clear is that we need "odd carers for odd kids". What is wrong with teenagers who feel that they are gay being placed with properly assessed gay couples? Or single people who can offer an enormous amount of attention to a damaged child without threatening other family relationships or jeopardising natural or other children in the family?'

He believes that there should be equal opportunities for all types of carer, just as there are equal opportunities policies for workers.

But however unprejudiced the individual social worker, local authority or adoption agency, public outcry against unusual adopters and the damage that does to the whole adoption process is often weighed against individual gain.

In the case of unmarried couples and single parent adopters – particularly women – this prejudice is disintegrating. However, such adopters are often more closely questioned and their personalities assessed for motivation much more than conventional couples. For them, the hurdles leading to adoption are made harder and higher.

However, the advantages of unusual adopters are beginning to be seen by some agencies. Today, a single person can be the adoptive parent of choice perhaps because they can offer more attention to a disabled child or because of a child's history – for instance, in the case of a girl who has been abused by her father and has an inherent distrust and dislike of men.

'The sad truth is that difficult-to-place children and unusual adopters spend the most time waiting to find each other,' said one seasoned adopter, 'but unfortunately time is one thing children don't have an endless amount of.'

• • •

Adoption without marriage

We are a couple who have successfully adopted without getting married and hope our experience will encourage others to contemplate this step.

Strictly speaking, we did not adopt as a couple, because legally this cannot be done unless you are married. Only married couples or single people can adopt under the present Adoption Act. The reason usually given for this is that if an unmarried couple splits up there is no clear legal machinery to establish matters such as guardianship or maintenance of children.

To overcome this problem, the agency through which we adopted required us to construct a legal agreement resembling the marriage contract but leaving out those parts not relevant to the welfare of children. We were also required to draw up wills providing for the guardianship and maintenance of our child in the event of either or both of our deaths.

Our adoption of a six-week-old, perfectly normal mixed-parentage baby went through quickly and smoothly. She is now three years old, bright, healthy and in every way delightful.

There are no legal barriers to the adoption of a child by an unmarried person, whether cohabiting or not, but many authorities evidently feel that there ought to be, and one hears of pressure being applied on unmarried couples to 'tie the knot'.

We would urge adoption agencies to consider the following. Marriage simply for the sake of adoption is a sham – people are no different because they have signed in front of witnesses. It does not guarantee anything. What it may do is force those with reservations about the marriage contract, whether of a personal or philosophical kind, to act hypocritically and end up feeling resentful and uncomfortable about being married.

Agencies might believe that married couples are more stable than unmarried ones. This is highly questionable, and even if it is true it is an attitude which puts excessive stress on a particular notion of stability. While married couples may exhibit a greater tendency to hang together when all desire to do so has gone, as a result of either family/social pressure or the sheer inconvenience and expense of getting a divorce, a dead relationship artificially maintained by an embarrassing legal contract is hardly the ideal setting in which to bring up children. Relationships between adults based on physical attraction combined with whatever else one finds admirable in the other person simply don't always have an indefinite lifetime. The child–adult parental type of relationship tends to outlive them. An adoption is far more likely than a marriage to mean 'till death do us part'.

In all cases the actual people and their circumstances should matter, not their marital status. We think any tendency to restrict less conventional applicants to difficult-to-place children should be strongly resisted. The conventional model is surely not so wonderful that its palest exemplar can outshine any imaginable alternative?

What is the real reason for some agencies' and authorities' insistence on marriage? In the case of a religious-based agency the reason is perhaps understandable, but in the case of a secular body we wonder if it stems from anything more than a hankering after 'respectability' of the most empty kind.

The single man

I am a single man and two years ago I replied to an advertisement placed by social services, who were trying to find a home for a 14-year-old boy who had been in a children's home for five years. To cut a long story short, I was assessed to adopt this boy, the assessment was successful and I met him for the first time eight months after seeing the advertisement. Two months later he moved in to live with me full-time. We are still going strong, I'm pleased to say!

During my assessment, I was concerned about the difficulties of school holidays and the fact that my adopted son would be home before me on school days, as I am in full-time employment. The assessing social worker's view was that there were practical difficulties, but she was sure I could make suitable arrangements; and in any case, was this not a lot better than what he had in the children's home? A very positive approach and, as it turned out, correct.

I hope that this encourages other single men who want to adopt not to give up and to find an agency with a positive approach. I also hope they know what they are letting themselves in for – the rewards are enormous but it is achieved at a cost. The adopter has to be prepared for his work to suffer sometimes, for which he is subsequently criticised. An understanding employer is nearly as important as the support and back-up of family, friends and neighbours.

Adoption by choice

We decided to adopt children without attempting to have babies and met with a suspicious reaction from many social services departments. We first approached our local social services to be short-term foster parents. This presented no problem: we were approved for children under 11 and were immediately asked to take two boys of 12 and 14.

A year later we asked about adoption and it was only then that our 'childlessness' became an issue. Our poor social worker got terribly embarrassed before eventually asking us whether we had a sexual problem; we assured her we had not and that it was moral principle that motivated us. We persuaded her that 'coming to terms with childlessness' was not a relevant issue for us unless we were turned down by everybody.

We confounded the image of the 'normal family' still further by insisting that I would continue to work full-time while my husband would become the homemaker. We had already experimented successfully with this system as foster parents, and at the time that the adoption panel turned us down we actually had in our care three foster children aged thirteen, four and three who were quite happy being cared for in this way. Obviously there was one set of rules for foster parents and quite another for would-be adopters! However, we refused to be deterred, at this stage joining Adoption UK and sending out letters to all neighbouring local authorities. We responded to an *Adoption UK Journal* feature on some girls, and although their particular circumstances made it inappropriate to proceed the contacts thus established enabled us to be put in touch with another social worker who was trying to place children. Within four months our sons, then aged four and six, were placed with us!

From our initial application until finding our children took about 18 months, much of which consisted of waiting for decisions – not an easy time – and trying to present our case to a faceless panel whom we would never meet.

Two years on we have added a 12-year-old girl to our family, this time as a result of a direct response to an *Adoption UK Journal* feature. On this occasion the issue of biological children did not arise. I don't know whether this is because it was already covered in our files, or whether it no longer applies now we have the boys.

Persistence paid off. It forced social workers to take us seriously and to have to try to justify their decisions.

The single woman – never take no for an answer

My daughter is now 11 and has been living with me for two years. But it was six years ago that I first enquired about adoption.

I had numerous disappointments before my daughter was placed with me, including being rejected by my home county as an adoptive parent one and a half years after my original enquiry and after only two visits from my social worker. Although this was not put in writing, I was told that as a single woman I was being 'greedy' in wanting a child for myself! But I was determined not to give up.

I was interviewed by three more boroughs and rejected. In the meantime I was applying for children from the *Adoption UK Journal*, *Foster Care* and *Be My Parent*. My daughter was publicised in *Foster Care* and I applied for her and received a letter saying that social workers were interested but would like to try local applicants first. 'The same old story,' I thought, and dismissed the matter.

But at the end of May I received another letter, this time saying that the other people were unsuitable and that they would like to see me. I travelled up the next day to meet the social workers. I was still positive that this was what I wanted when I returned, so I was overjoyed when on the day of my fortieth birthday, I received a letter from this local authority saying that they would like to proceed.

Everything else proceeded very quickly and in the summer holiday I met my daughter for the first time. We got on with each other instantly. I then went on a previously arranged holiday for two weeks, but when I returned I stayed near the children's home for a week and took my daughter out. The following week, her children's home came down to my part of the country for their holiday and I picked up my daughter so that she could spend a few days with me. Two weeks later she was placed with me.

Since then we have, of course, had many ups and downs, and being on my own sometimes makes it more difficult. However, the advantages certainly outweigh the disadvantages and I wouldn't be without my daughter for the world. She has changed considerably since being here, getting rid of the many bad habits she arrived with and becoming settled and much calmer. When I look back on what she was like last year, I can hardly believe it's the same child, although this year there have been different problems – this, I'm told, is very normal! We flew to Canada this summer to visit my 93-year-old grandmother and my aunt and uncle. My daughter has now met all my family and been accepted by everyone. She had her birthday during this holiday, and the excitement of this together with the thrill of her first experience of air travel made for a memorable summer.

My daughter says: 'I am very happy living with mum because we live near the sea and the countryside. I am also able to have guinea pigs and we have a cat – I've never been able to have pets before. I like doing lots of activities (swimming, riding, Guides and drama club) which I've never done before. I sometimes think it would be nice to have a dad to play with, but if Mum did get married I'd always be worried that they might have arguments and would split up, so I don't really mind not having a dad.'

I would say to all other single people who are trying to adopt: Persevere… and never take no for an answer.

Getting through the assessment

I had always longed for a child but assumed that as a single woman it would be virtually impossible to adopt. Three years ago I met Lucy, a single woman who had adopted two boys with Down's syndrome. She appeared to have faced little difficulty in being accepted as a single adopter, having been chosen for her second son in preference to several married couples.

After thinking things over carefully I contacted an adoption agency. My desire for a very young child, together with a long-standing interest in people with learning difficulties, naturally led me to consider a baby with Down's syndrome.

I was told by an adoption agency that babies with Down's syndrome were very popular and that I had little hope of adopting one under two, but they did agree to start an assessment. Early on, however, we ran into problems as the social worker, questioning me closely on my background and family, seized on every negative point and magnified it out of all proportion. A friend assessed by the same man had the same experience. After four months of searching interviews the agency finally rejected my application.

With dwindling hopes I tried another agency, only to be asked if they could contact the agency that had turned me down in order to ask them the reasons. This seemed very unfair. I had no intention of concealing any facts but the reasons my social worker had given for rejecting me were largely based on his subjective assessment of my personality.

Just as I felt like giving up I talked again with Lucy, who encouraged me to keep on trying and told me that she had heard that our local county council were looking for a home for a baby boy with Down's syndrome.

When I telephoned the baby's social worker she eagerly followed up my enquiry with a visit. Within six months I was approved with virtually no difficulty. Although I had to mention my prior rejection, my new social worker seemed to take a very different view of my personality. In fact, I heard that the only real matter of concern to the panel was how I would cope with the drop in income, having been used to an actuary's salary. My social worker managed to convince them that this would not be a major problem and phoned me to say, 'Congratulations! You've got a son.' Three weeks later, after several visits to his foster home, I brought my son home. Although by then he was 13 months old, he settled down immediately and soon made progress. When he first came to me he could not sit up, but now, at two and a half, he is walking, feeding himself and saying several words. He is a great joy to me and now I'm looking for a little brother or sister for him, preferably another child with Down's syndrome.

Update 1999: Six years ago Michael, who also has Down's syndrome, joined the family at the age of six months. Life is very busy with two lively boys, especially now that I have gone back to work part-time, but I wouldn't change a thing.

A lesbian adoption

I always wanted kids. Kids had always kind of figured in my life. I had presumed that I would have to do something biological about it and had not got around to it for all sorts of reasons. Having a child biologically is really an issue for lesbian couples. Only one of you can be the biological parent. In this sense adoption is much more equal.

When I got together with my partner we both wanted children and we both wanted to be equally involved, which was very important to us. Adoption seemed the right option for us – why bring kids into an awful world when there are a number of kids here already who need parenting? For us there was a lot of logic in adopting kids rather than having them biologically. But the decision to adopt was also to do with the time in our lives when we made the decision and our perspective as a couple. We wanted to bring up children and this seemed the right avenue.

The first problem was in finding an authority to assess us. We rang lots of London authorities and most of the time they weren't interested. One even said we had to be married! They had not understood what they were being asked at all. We told every authority we approached that we were a lesbian couple. We felt it was right to be completely open about that from the start.

Eventually, one authority did take us on. It didn't take that long – we made an application in the September and by the November were on a course. We were lucky. There is a Lesbian and Gay Foster and Adoptive Parents Network (LAGFAPN) and through that we learned which authorities might be sympathetic to our application. The Network has been a very useful support group and resource.

We did not want to be pioneers. We just wanted to adopt children and felt we had something to offer. Some authorities are beginning to realise that alternative sorts of families like ours might be better families in certain situations for kids with very difficult backgrounds. We needed to find an authority that understood that we had something very positive to offer to children both as individuals and as a couple. Unusual children sometimes need unusual parents.

We were assessed over the following 12 months and went to panel the next April – but it wasn't until September three and half years later that our girls were finally placed with us for adoption.

It was a long haul – we just had to keep writing and writing letters. First, we had to wait for a year to see if the authority we had been approved by could link us with children, but they didn't. Then we started to apply for children we saw in the *Adoption UK Journal* and *Be My Parent*. I reckon I wrote over 100 letters. And then of course there were the phone calls – endless phone calls. Very occasionally, we would get a letter back saying thank you for your letter, very sorry.

Our friends could not believe how determined we were. But by the end it was getting pretty awful. I am an optimistic person but I began to worry that somehow we had managed to miss the boat. We weren't getting anywhere. We had numerous calls and visits from social workers. It is the social workers in the end that make or break a match. We would get very hopeful each time only to be faced with a disappointment. We had five visits that just went nowhere.

But things got better all of a sudden. We were linked tentatively with a child in West London and we actually went to see her. It was an older girl and we met her social worker and foster parents and visited her school, where we saw her in her classroom and our hearts went out to her. We had wanted to adopt a sibling group but she seemed right for us. Then the authority began to get cold feet.

At that same time we were approached about a bigger group of four younger children by someone with whom we had talked before. After some discussion we decided to find out more about these children, and told the first authority what was happening. We just didn't want to lose everything and face rejection from the first authority and lose these other children.

We had become more sceptical altogether by this time, so after the initial conversation we did not jump around and say, yes, yes. We went off on holiday – a long holiday trundling around China. The day we got back we received a phone call from the social worker, who wanted to talk to us more about these four children. In the end we referred to her as our fairy godmother. She fought our corner so strongly and without her we wouldn't have got anywhere. They were four school-age girls and we felt that they were right for us and we were right for them.

It still took time but when we finally heard that we were approved for these four we had a night at home with a good friend and one of our parents clinking glasses of sparkling wine. It was the summer. Everything went quickly and we wanted to get the children moved in by September, ready to start school. I remember we were putting beds up and getting ready until three o'clock in the morning the night before they arrived.

That's all a few years ago now. In the years since there have been many difficult times and also many enjoyable times when we have felt like an ordinary family.

CHAPTER 9

Adoption and Race

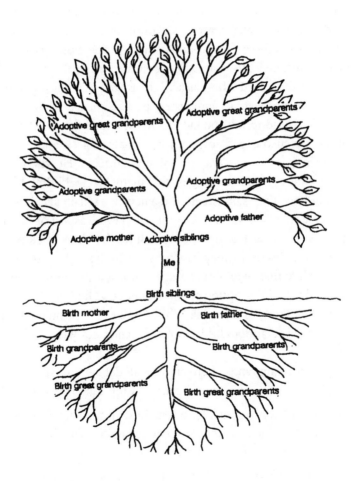

Race is a sensitive and emotive subject in any context. The issue of adoption and same-race placements has for a number of years been at the centre of much outraged and uncomfortable discussion amongst potential adopters, adoptive families, the social work profession and the media.

There are two extremes of opinion and many variations in between. One is that same-race placements are of paramount importance and the other is that they are irrelevant, though most opinion within Adoption UK falls somewhere between the two.

The problem is aggravated by two issues. The first is the race imbalance in Britain between children needing adoption and potential adopters. A small but growing proportion of potential adopters are from racially mixed, black and Asian families, but a much larger proportion of the children who need new families come from these backgrounds. White people hoping to adopt can feel particularly frustrated by what others consider to be their 'unsuitability' to adopt a mixed-race child who has a white as well as a black parent.

Second, the problem is aggravated by the recent complete change of national policy on adoption and race. Until the end of the 1970s white couples were positively encouraged to adopt mixed-race, black and Asian children. This was seen as a positive way of 'mixing' all races. However, by the early 1980s there was evidence to suggest that many black children brought up in white families had little self-esteem and a negative self-image. It was sad proof of the extremes to which racism has permeated every aspect of our lives – from subconscious racism such as describing a child's hands as black when they are dirty to blatant discriminatory practices by individuals and institutions. A change of policy that would encourage black and racially mixed families to come forward into the adoption arena (families that had previously often been discouraged) was seen as essential. White families who would have previously been encouraged to adopt children of different races were no longer seen as suitable.

In the continuing and often emotional debate on adoption and race Adoption UK has steered a central course. Adoption UK believes that:

- When children are unable to remain with their families of birth it is in their best interests that alternative families which reflect their original culture and background should be sought wherever possible.

- Strenuous efforts to achieve this aim should be positively and warmly supported.

- Time to achieve this aim must be limited. The needs of individual children must be borne in mind. If at the end of an agreed period of energetic and well-documented effort a suitable same-race family has not been found, the child should be placed with the best family available. This may mean placement across racial lines with families who have positive views about becoming a racially-mixed unit and the ability to achieve it whatever the racial/cultural background of the parents.

- There should be full and ongoing support for established racially mixed adoptive families.

Adoption UK remains convinced that to remain parentless is an impediment few survive without deep scars – and that 'perfect' parents sadly do not exist anyway.

But the thoughts of adopters and adoptees on this subject speak louder than any theory. For many it isn't just the parenting but the attitudes of schools and friends that can make or break a transracial adoption. Developing a black or mixed-race child's pride in his or her heritage and helping that child to develop a sense of self-esteem have to be vigorously and unflaggingly pursued, particularly if the child is adopted across racial lines.

As one young man of mixed race, brought up by a very loving white family, said: 'There were a number of occasions in my childhood when my dark complexion and foreign name evoked reactions from people.

It would have been helpful if I could have discussed the problems I experienced on account of my racial background with one of my parents.'

He concludes that it is crucial for mixed-race people in Britain to gain confidence in themselves and that this is easier to achieve in a family of similar background. However, like most others in favour of same-race placements, he believes that a child should not lose the potential security of an adoptive family because no same-race parent comes forward.

Here are the views of some adopters and adoptees caught up in the adoption and race debate.

• • •

A transracial family

We are a transracial family consisting of two white parents (second-generation Jewish immigrants), one white daughter, one mixed-parentage white and Afro-Caribbean daughter and one black Afro-Caribbean son.

This is the story of how we began to damage our second child psychologically, and how we overcame this and now believe that our child will be happy despite having been brought up by white parents. By the age of four

our daughter was wishing to be white, and was asking questions like, 'Why is black magic bad and white magic good?,' and was always talking about colour, which we as white liberals found difficult to discuss, as we had been brought up to believe that all children were the same. These are the steps we gradually learnt we had to take:

1. We learnt to talk about the colour of people and not to dismiss it. This helped our child to feel that there was nothing shameful about being black, and she started telling us of racial incidents.

2. We learnt to do her hair and skin properly. Dry, unkempt or very short hair is the main indicator that a child is transracially adopted. If you find it too difficult, then go to a black hairdresser (though this can be very expensive and time consuming). This is so important – if her hair is not done properly, a girl will feel ugly and have very low self-esteem.

3. We only send our children to schools and clubs which are predominantly black and have black adults. The children then have natural relationships with other black children and adults and will absorb their language and culture. Our children will not be called 'bounty' or 'coconut', as other transracially adopted children are, because they fit in.

4. Most importantly, we subscribe to a black newspaper. You won't find news about black people in the white press unless it's negative.

Our daughter is still different from her friends in that she is not a Christian and hasn't been brought up in an authoritarian way, and they are shocked at her lack of respect when we argue and banter! However, she is well armed with information to survive within the black community. She has to be, as that is where she firmly belongs. After all, even though we are educated, middle-class whites and she comes from a very academic, middle-class black family, she was still stereotyped at secondary school, and was once told off for making 'West Indian faces'!

Even though we believe our black children have strong black identities, we still believe in same-race placements. In every new situation our children enter, they have to explain about adoption and why they have white parents, and they have had to learn how to fend off embarrassing, probing questions from children and adults. Many transracial adopters feel the same way as we do, but unfortunately the media like to see this as a black/white conflict and are not interested in our views. Same-race placements are here to stay and should be accepted as being in the best interests of the child, which is what adoption is all about.

How could I say no?

Tiny little fingers curling into mine
Black fingers, brown fingers, delicate and fine.
Large eyes look at me, round and dark they glow,
'Are you going to read to me?' How could I say no?

Black hair, curly hair, hair as straight as rain,
Fuzzy hair, silky hair, to brush and brush again.
Long legs, jumping feet, running to and fro,
'Are you going to come with me?' How could I say no?

All the different colours given us to see,
Make a glorious picture, a bit of it is me,
And you are all a part of it, white or black and so
'Are you going to love them all?' How could I say no?

By Jill Sturdy, mother and adoptive mother of 12 children

Transracial adoption: The danger of oversimplification

I am the son of a white English mother and an Indian father. My parents separated before I was two and subsequently I was brought up by my mother and my white grandmother. Throughout my childhood I had no contact with my father or members of his family. I am now 32 and the adoptive father of two mixed-race children.

Although I was not adopted, I was a mixed-race child brought up by white people. My attitude to the doctrine of racial compatibility in adoption is consequently based on the experience of my own childhood.

There were a number of occasions in my childhood when my dark complexion and foreign name evoked reactions from people. These ranged from enquiries about my background to derision and abuse. The enquiries were generally made by adults, especially schoolteachers, and the derision and abuse usually came from my peers. In all cases I suffered considerable distress. It is understandable how any child would suffer if he or she were to become the object of vindictive abuse from school bullies. In my case it was generally my racial background that was the object of the bullies' invective. However, school bullies also victimise white children on a whole gamut of pretexts.

In retrospect what I find significant is that I was also distressed when my racial origins were the object of dispassionate, well-meaning enquiry. I clearly had no pride in my Asian background and I tried to persuade people that I had no Asian blood in me.

I remember trying to conceal my dark complexion by avoiding white fluorescent light, which made it look darker, and endeavouring to show people the palms of my hands wherever possible rather than the darker backs. It is not surprising that I grew to hate my name and the dark skin which went with it.

Why did I repeatedly feel the need to deny and conceal my Asian background, often when I was under no threat of racist abuse? I simply did not want to be different from my peers, virtually all of whom were white. There were a few Asian children at my school, from whom I was completely alienated. This was because their culture was so utterly different from my own. They spoke to each other in Punjabi or Urdu and dressed in ways which I found strange. I identified with the culture of my white peers but my name and the colour of my skin made many people assume that my culture must be that of the other Asian people.

My mother and grandmother rarely thought about the Asian element of my background and I felt inhibited from talking to them about the problems I was facing.

The crucial problem faced by mixed-race people in England is having confidence in themselves as individuals. Whereas the majority of white English people may accept them as completely English there will always be a minority who will regard them as different, in some cases without bearing any malice, in others out of fear or hatred of anything foreign. The mixed-race person has to have the self-esteem to give him or her resilience against the knocks that he or she is likely to receive from the society with whose culture he or she identifies.

But my lack of self-confidence does not only relate to my racial background. Although the ideal would have been to have been brought up by mixed-race parents, the crucial factor which broke my self-esteem and my resilience against the knocks that my racial background entails was the disturbance of losing my father in early childhood.

I am convinced that it is better for an adopted child to be placed in a stable but racially incompatible family than for him or her to suffer emotional trauma in early childhood on account of being kept in an institution or wrenched from parents with whom he or she has bonded. A stable upbringing from a very early age with racially incompatible parents will grant the child far more resilience and ability to cope with English society than an unstable childhood.

What a difference a school makes

Our adopted mixed-race son and daughter, Henry and Leah, have changed enormously since we moved them from the largely white, middle-class primary schools they used to attend to their present junior school at the Asian/white working-class end of town.

Eighteen months ago Leah was involved in a road accident and her leg was broken. Out of hospital and back home but still in considerable pain, she announced that she was glad she had broken her leg because now we couldn't send her back to school. We were finally confronted with a stark example of how unhappy school was making our children and we decided to find other schools which might make them less unhappy.

We had always known that Henry's school experiences were far from ideal, but to some extent we took the blame for this ourselves. He is our middle one, our first son, our first adopted black child and the victim of all our early naivety and inexperience. As he progressed through primary school he become (in term-time) more and more withdrawn, reticent and hostile. He seemed to be 'unlearning' rather than learning. He had arrived in the infants' class able to read but now seemed to find it impossible to concentrate. He was sent to remedial classes and we were told he had to develop a thicker skin to survive the jibes of other children. The school's attitude to him seemed to be that he was a difficult if occasionally charming little boy with educational problems.

We had always felt we had done better with Leah. From the beginning we actively encouraged her to identify herself proudly as black. She blazed forth confidently in the world of playgroup and primary school like a small comet. Fiery, fierce, unstoppable Leah.

She had rarely complained about name-calling or bullying or indeed given any sign of her unhappiness. Now I understand that she didn't complain because she had no words for the lonely, humiliating experience of feeling 'wrong', an experience which as white parents we could not apparently share or protect her from. She also felt that her school troubles were in some way her own fault.

I need a book to describe how the new school differs from the first. It would be easy to assume that Henry and Leah found acceptance and happiness because they now go to school alongside lots of other children like themselves, but this is not in fact true. Henry and Leah's natural fathers were Afro-Caribbean. About three-quarters of their new friends come from various parts of Asia, including Vietnam.

The success of the school lies in the loving, open and courageous approach of the staff and headmistress. Without this embracing attitude and tough common sense, the multicultural books and artefacts and the observation of Divali, Eid and Chinese New Year would all be so much window dressing. The headmistress said she couldn't promise that Henry and Leah wouldn't meet the same difficulties in the playground as before, but if and when this happened school policy was to talk about it and learn from it.

Henry and Leah's ex-headteachers told us they never regarded them as black, and it was clear that they regarded this as the most positive and compassionate attitude. The effect of this silent politeness was to make Henry and Leah feel discounted, helpless and powerless.

In his first week at his new school Henry found himself in the novel position of explaining away his white mum and dad to a curious and slightly antagonistic group of Asian boys. His teacher promptly turned the lesson over to the issues of colonialism, slavery, and the immigration of West Indians to Britain in the 1950s. When Henry came home he repeated word for word what he remembered. He was shining with enthusiasm. He had been named. He belonged.

At the end of the first term at his new school, using some of his precious Christmas money, Henry had one of his ears pierced to hold a small gold stud. This was not enthusiastically received by some friends and neighbours, but we were delighted, for this was a little boy who had spent years trying to become invisible, a background child suddenly deciding to be visible – and celebrating it in style.

Being part of a multiracial family

I am mixed race (of West Indian and English origin). I was adopted by my white English parents when I was five weeks and five days old. My family is a melting pot in itself. We range from the white, blond-haired, blue-eyed type to the totally black West Indian to the half-St Helenian/half-Maltese.

The main way in which adoption by white parents and being brought up on the predominantly white South Coast has affected me was brought to my attention recently. A friend on the same degree course as myself remarked upon the fact that in comparison with other black people I show a much greater ability and willingness to mix with white and black people alike. At polytechnic most black students socialise exclusively together, study together and minimise their contact with whites. I am free from many of the restrictive prejudices that young black people still carry around with them.

A lot of this may be due to the fact that my parents are very open-minded concerning questions of race.

Being mixed race I share in that almost legendary instant rapport between black people, yet having been brought up by white parents it is perfectly ordinary and easy for me to have great friends who are white. I cross the race boundaries uninhibitedly. It frightens me to think that if I were a child requiring a placement at the present time, expressed or implied current adoption agency attitudes would mean that I would not be placed for adoption with my present parents. This attitude turns the supposed 'helper' into the child's worst enemy. If there are people in the community who do not place unnecessary importance upon issues of pigmentation, they should be seriously considered as appropriate people to adopt children of different races. Suitability is not solely a question of colour. British society itself is irrevocably mixed: transracial adoption seems to be a logical extension of this which can help harmonise racial combination.

The rights of black children

I am a mixed race adult who was brought up entirely among white children and adults. I only knew my white mother and as a result found it very hard throughout childhood explaining to children and adults how my mother was white and I was brown. I appreciate that times have changed and that white families have in general become more sensitive to children's needs in a multicultural society; the fact remains, however, that your colour can be everything, and is very important to you as you are developing. Of course we should teach our children to see everyone as equal and colour as not important in judging others, but anyone who believes same-race placements are 'mostly a load of rubbish', should be aware that they are treading on dangerous ground.

To an extent, children can be successfully adopted and grow well in loving white families, but it has to be remembered that the policy of same-race placements did not evolve overnight. It has been a natural progression and a healthy affirmation of black children's rights. Perhaps people are not aware that for a black couple to adopt a white child would once have been almost unheard of.

As a parent of three adopted and two natural children, I often flick through the 'Children who wait' pages of the *Adoption UK Journal*. I see many white children, and ask myself why I would not apply to adopt one of them. The answer is obvious. Yes, they are lovely children and no doubt I would be a good mother, but would it be fair to that blond-haired, blue-eyed child to bring her into our family? Of course she would grow up more accepting of black people as the result of living in a black family, but it would pose problems for her in later life. At the end of the day I heartily recommend that as far as possible children are placed according to their racial identity.

Two of my adopted mixed-race children suffered severe problems integrating into our lifestyle, as they had been placed in white foster households prior to the adoption placement. Even the simple task of plaiting hair became a terrible battleground. Even to this day our youngest is sensitive about her colour, as no work was done on identity previously. She has the most beautiful black features and bushy dark curls. We have been subtly encouraging to her about her colour, as she did not like being referred to as 'brown' or 'black' when first placed at six years old. On holiday she was playing alone outside the chalet and I watched as she was approached by a girl of her own age. 'Are you a blackie?' the girl asked. My heart went out to my daughter as I saw her hesitate before answering, 'Of course not, I'm like you.' With one statement this innocent playmate was ramming home her negative perception of blackness.

Having said all this, as black adopters are not as many in number as their white counterparts, I believe that white families can provide happy homes for many of our children. The trend must be, though, towards same-race placement. Colour is not so much physical attribute as life experiences and inherited tradition.

CHAPTER 10

Openness in Adoption

Openness in adoption is the about-face in the world of adoption which has given pain, pleasure and greater understanding to adoptees, adopters and birth families in the past 20 years.

In 1976, after years of secrecy, the law changed. This change gave adult adoptees access to their original birth certificates, enabling them to trace their birth relatives. Within a few years opinion had swung towards altogether more openness in adoption. Many felt this was consolidated by the Children's Act of 1989, under which the court can make an order for 'contact' with the birth family at the same time as it makes an adoption order under the 1976 Adoption Act.

Some link – however tenuous – between an adoptee and his or her birth family is now believed to be of benefit not only to the adoptee, whose past becomes a reality that can be dealt with, but also to the birth family, who formerly had not the faintest idea of the outcome of adoption for the child they had to part with. Openness can also help adopters to better understand the nature of the child they are nurturing.

'It was a positive move for all concerned,' said one experienced adopter who regrets the lack of openness in the adoption of her two children. 'An adopted child is never an open book to their adoptive parents. You know the ordinary things, like they won't eat fish and they're good at art. Life story books help fill in some of the past. But there are always going to be parts of the puzzle missing – both for the adopter and the adoptee. Some openness in adoption can help to make the picture clearer for all involved.'

Today, comparatively few adoptions take place in which all lines of communication between the birth family and the adoptive family are cut permanently. The extent of openness ranges enormously and at its best is planned according to each child's case and changes as time passes according to the developing needs of all parties, particularly those of the adopted child. Sometimes the only form of contact is through a 'letter box' system run by an adoption or social work service for occasional exchange of information and Christmas and birthday cards.

For many older children placed at a later age, greater openness and contact with their birth families is almost inevitable. Many know only too well where their parents, grandparents and siblings are living, and although they may not wish to contact their parents, their extended family can be important to them.

Openness does not mean constant or even infrequent contact with a birth family. 'Contact has to be handled very carefully and very individually. Openness means that rather than bricking up the door to a child's past and pretending it never existed, you may close and even lock the door but everyone knows where the key is so that when and if it becomes necessary or desirable for the door to be opened again, even only slightly, then that can be achieved,' said one adopter.

Adopters believe that the degree of openness and contact must vary with the families to whom it applies. A survey of members by Adoption UK showed one significant theme emerging from all adopters: a plea for flexibility and for individual circumstances to be taken into account when determining the amount, frequency and type of contact. Many adopters confessed that they found it easier to maintain contact with 'significant' other people from their child's family than immediate birth parents, and many preferred non-physical contact – photos and letters – rather than meetings.

For all concerned there is sometimes an underlying fear of face-to-face contact. For adopters it is a fear rooted in the subconscious belief that perhaps the child will prefer the birth parent and the birth parent will want the child back. For the child it's a fear of rejection or abandonment, or both. And for the birth parent it's a fear of dragging up a past they hadn't been able to cope with.

Today, with the general trend towards more openness in adoption, more and more adopters wish they knew more about their child's birth family, and often seek out links to help their child piece together his or her lost history. Once an adoptee reaches the age of 18, he or she is free to decide whether or not to make contact with this birth family, though in practice many don't feel ready to do so until their mid-twenties or thirties, if at all. It is accepted that some openness in adoption helps to dispel illusions on all sides and allows a child to move forward in life.

As one adoptive mother says: 'You have to know and understand your family roots. It is difficult to have a future without having had a past.'

● ● ●

Their need to know (real names used)

Our little boys, aged five and seven, have just met their birth mother. It has been a wonderful experience for all concerned.

Maria came to London from Italy at 19, already using heroin regularly, and knowing no one. The next six years were to prove chaotic and distressing, with no settled jobs, accommodation or relationships. Nor could she depend upon support in Italy, where she had spent ten years from the age of three in a large institution. Maria gave birth to two sons and both were removed within a few days of birth because of Maria's severe psychiatric illness. Josh came to us at ten months.

We heard that Maria was pregnant again. Knowing from our social worker that her mental state was no better, we expressed our wish for the new baby to come to us if a family were needed so that the children could grow up together. Michael joined our family at five months. Maria never accepted the adoption plan and had not wished to meet us, but she didn't actually contest the adoption applications. She returned to Italy.

Some months later Maria sent two lovely tracksuits for the boys via the London borough that had placed them. We were happy about this and it was the start of regular, although infrequent, contact in the form of birthday cards, letters and gifts, using the borough as a postbox.

When Josh was six, he began to express sadness and regret that he didn't know Maria or her little daughter Maddalena, born on her return to Italy and now two. He also wondered how she was. 'She's probably still sad because she gave us up,' Josh told me, voicing his thoughts. He also said: 'She probably cried when she had Maddalena because it made her remember giving up me and Anthony.'

We were aware that for Josh, although he was happy and settled with us, a central piece of the jigsaw was missing. We went to see a senior social worker, bounced around some ideas and came away having resolved to ask Maria if she would like to meet my wife.

We wrote and Maria said she would love to meet. They were delighted to see each other and hugged and talked for hours.

Several months later I took the boys to Italy. Quite simply, it was a marvellous experience. It felt so *right*, seeing the boys with Maria and Maddalena, watching the quiet happiness and easy, loving contact between them all.

It is important to mention also the little pangs I felt once or twice, like on the first day when Anthony took Maria's hand as we went walking, and when he said 'bye Mum' as we parted that evening. But generally it was a really good feeling and profoundly moving to watch the four of them together and to recognise that they shared something very special which didn't include me.

After two and a half very full days we said goodbye to Maria at Milan Station. I felt very warm towards her. I said it must be hard losing the boys again. She answered firmly that she was happy the boys were living with us. As the train pulled out Michael settled down and went to sleep; Josh was very sad, sobbing deeply, more upset than I have ever seen him. For him, the visit was so short after wanting it for so long. I felt very close to him in his distress, and was glad that he was able to express such deep feelings.

Some friends worried that the trip would unsettle the boys. It has done quite the reverse. They slipped back happily into life at home. They have gained something immeasurable. We are going on holiday to Italy this summer and our other sons will meet our new Italian family. We hope Maria and Maddalena will, one day, come to stay with us.

Update 1999: Looking back, seven years on, we're very glad this all happened when the boys were so young, because it's been much easier for them to assimilate all the subsequent contacts with Maria, her relatives and both birth fathers. Had they been older we feel it could have been more awkward for them.

A special family

We have come full circle in our view of open adoption. We never envisaged any type of contact with the natural family when we were first approved, but eventually started to realise that such contact can be a very positive thing, especially for an older child. It gives the child the assurance that the new family accepts the natural family as something good. Everyone likes to think that their family is special and that is true even for the child who may not have had much parenting in earlier years.

Our eldest child is almost 16 and we have contact with five older half-siblings. We also correspond twice a year with the natural father. We all live in the same town, so we meet when shopping etc. Our son left his birth family at the age of four and a half due to his mother's death. Prior to her death he had been in and out of care. The father remarried but the child did not fit in with the new family. During all his time in residential care the half-siblings maintained contact and they, particularly the two older girls, were the only stable thing in his life.

We have contact three times a year with our youngest child's half-siblings, but the contact does not mean a great deal to her at present. The half-siblings, 11 and 9 years old, definitely gain from the contact with her.

We can understand the fear of having contact. In the final analysis it comes down to the families involved. If possible, contact should be arranged between the adoptive parents and the natural parents without social workers being present. Natural families, like adoptive families, are uneasy, and the unspoken question of 'Will it be okay?' will be there until trust grows between the two families. We hope any new legislation will allow for flexibility and accept that contact is not possible in all cases.

Who's the lucky one?

I love our little girl very much. I want her to develop into a well-adjusted adult who is comfortable with the fact of her adoption. We have exchanged many letters and photographs with her birth parents and are pleased to hear their news. It did take me some time to get used to the fact that our correspondence had been read by at least two social workers and one photocopyist before it reached us!

I feel very guilty when I think of the birth family's pain. I know that my daughter's birth mother is finding it hard to come to terms with her loss. Sometimes I wonder whether she would like to resume the care of the daughter she gave birth to. Some people may assume that the fact that I even consider this shows that I haven't really claimed my daughter as my own. Perhaps they could advise me on how I should overcome these feelings of guilt; after all, I'm one of the lucky ones – we do have a child.

The meeting we had with our daughter's birth parents was a good experience. They talked of their hopes and wishes for her future, their views on religion and family lifestyle. They were both confident that we would give her the kind of life they wished for her. Of course, there were tears from us all but both birth parents expressed their relief that someone was willing to take on responsibility for the child – a responsibility that they felt unwilling and unable to assume.

It was the professionals who constantly referred to the grief, the loss and the pain. It was the professionals who asked us to imagine how the birth father's parents would feel to have had only sons and now be losing their first granddaughter to us. It was the professionals who wouldn't allow us to tell the birth parents of the name we had chosen to add to her original names for fear of upsetting them still further.

My concern is that many adoptive parents are unsure whether they are being asked to be parents or guardians. This level of insecurity must affect the children in their care. Many adoptive parents fear that one day retrospective legislation may be brought in which allows them to be contacted by birth parents at any time. After all, women who relinquished a child years ago and who have never told their families or husbands would fear the arrival on their doorstep of the child they gave up.

Stephanie's story

From my own experiences, I sincerely believe that if you tell a child the truth – within the limits of their understanding – about their background, they can come to terms with life. You have to know and understand your family roots. It is difficult to have a future without having had a past.

We had this thought in mind when we adopted our daughters.

Our adopted daughter Stephanie's birth mother had survived several doomed relationships, including marriages and widowhood, before settling down with Stephanie's father. Her previous four daughters had all been taken into care and adopted by another family. Unfortunately, Stephanie's mother lacked sufficient parenting skills and was unable to cope while the father was out at work. Eventually, Stephanie came into care and was placed with foster parents with a view to finding a suitable adoptive family. At this time Stephanie was two and a half years old. Her parents visited her at the foster home for six months until visits were terminated when she was three. Nine months later she was placed with us.

It was obvious that Stephanie's memories of her parents, particularly of her father, were still strong and very important to her. He asked his social worker if he could meet us and this was something we wanted to do.

The sight of that poor man sitting in a bleak social services office, knowing full well that he had been obliged to sign away his only child, the girl he had loved and cared for during the first two and half years of her life, was absolutely appalling. He was resigned to the fact that he could not give her the life he wanted her to have and he wanted her to have the best. We promised that we would do our utmost for her and that we would send him photos and progress reports via social services. We also promised that if ever she wanted to trace him when she was older we would give our total support and assistance. When the distress of the meeting became too much for him he got up and left in tears.

In the weeks that followed we became more and more certain that we should try to maintain contact with Stephanie's family where possible. Her older half-sisters remembered her well and, as we discovered later, were anxious to meet her.

Then that Christmas we had a heart-rending message via social services from Stephanie's paternal grandmother. Would we consider accepting birthday and Christmas presents for her?

Stephanie's widowed grandmother has no other grandchildren. When Stephanie was given up for adoption it was exactly as if she had gone missing. Unlike a death, where grief diminishes with the passage of time, not knowing the fate of a child is a constant lifelong heartache.

Our first meeting with 'Nanny' was remarkable. Stephanie not only remembered the house where she had spent many happy days as a toddler but also where various items were to be found.

We keep up the flow of photos and progress reports to Stephanie's 'first daddy', and she kept her memories by means of a beautiful life story book which he had begun for her in the months when she was in foster care so that we should never forget her roots.

We have met Stephanie's father again and her mother, and taken her to see her father at his mother's house. Stephanie is happy to know that her first mummy and daddy continue to love and care about her even though they cannot look after her. She feels wealthy in relatives.

Open adoption: Is it for everyone?

My wife and I have two children by birth, aged 12 and 11, and have adopted a brother and sister aged ten and eight who have the same birth mother but whose fathers are unknown. They were removed by the court due to an extremely negative home environment and a lack of parenting skills on their mother's part, and as a result they had severe emotional scars and behavioural problems.

After three and a half years in a children's home they were placed with us and have begun to make superb progress in all areas of life. The birth mother was against adoption, and when the event drew close she began a frantic effort to regain some control over them. She has made some progress in her life with the burden of the children lifted, and has established herself in business for her own future.

A goodbye visit had not been completed after the freeing order. The visit was finally scheduled recently and went as well as was possible. Gifts were exchanged, private time with mum was allowed for, and final goodbyes were said. The expected tears ran freely and words of acceptance of the new family were spoken. All the textbook ingredients went into the meeting and we were told we could expect some negative consequences. We had no idea how bad they would be.

The problems had really begun two months prior to the meeting. The children were excited and very scared. The biggest reaction had been one of fear that they would lose our love and that they would have to go back to mum, and we tried to demonstrate our commitment to them and give them assurances that they were secure in our family. They reverted to extreme disobedience and both lost years of development.

After the meeting, when the tears subsided, they had many more questions and demands. They had remembered a mum who could not care for them, shouted and slapped them, and who did not know how to take care of a house, feed them or teach them basic skills. They remembered severe poverty and being left alone for long periods. But they now met a bright and flashy mum who seemed to have finally got her act together. She was taking college classes and working full-time. She shared a flat with a friend and they were told she was doing great in all areas of her life. She was sweet to them and talked of the fun times they used to have when she pushed them on the swings and played with them on the slide. They had a good time with her and the sadness of having to leave this super mum was now so traumatic that they did not know how to feel. The trip back home was hard and the first question was: 'Why can't Mum take care of us now?'

Since the meeting the children have misbehaved and any punishment is seen as a lack of love. If they are told off they retreat to their room and pen a letter to their mum or to their old National Children's Homes (NCH) home.

We have dealt with each situation, showed love and patience, and demonstrated our commitment no matter what. They have finally started showing signs of returning affection and learning from discipline, but at a very slow rate. Each lesson seems to be tested and repeated daily.

This all leads me to view open adoption as something that is not for everyone. I feel that children must be free to settle the past in their own time, and that this type of artificial meeting can do far more harm than good.

The children's social workers had counselled them for years on starting a new life, and just when it seems to start they toss the old life back in their faces with changes that confuse them. The children were dealing with the emotional scars of their past until this severe interruption started. I have yet to see any positive reaction.

The conflicts facing them were too deep for their ages and emotional states and have caused extensive behavioural problems. They were not ready and they may not be ready until they reach adulthood.

An early open adoption

We first met our two adopted children with their mother. The eldest was then three and the youngest 18 months.

We were told that even if we went ahead with the adoption their birth mother would want to see the children again in the future. She herself had been in a children's home and was concerned that they should have the family life that she herself had not experienced.

Two months later the children came to live with us. For nearly two years the children remained in our care and, at her request, did not see their mother. The day before the adoption hearing we met in a park – she came with her boyfriend and the children's social worker. We talked and played with the children and had a snack in a nearby cafe. It was all very low-key.

At the adoption hearing the judge granted the mother reasonable access after an initial period of two years, during which time no meetings were to take place. This was her suggestion, as she reasoned the children should be given time to establish a relationship with us.

The next meeting didn't take place for nearly three years. We met at London Zoo. By that time we had another 'home-grown' child and she too had a two-year-old.

We met again at the zoo two years later. The meeting was a long one. The children investigated all the animals, played with each other and had shy conversations with their birth mother.

Several months later the youngest asked who her father was. We were unable to tell her and suggested she write to her birth mother. She had the reply almost by return of post. It was a most moving letter. Her birth mother said she could not answer the question because she did not know. She explained that the two children had been adopted because she 'could not give them a normal family with a mummy and daddy'. She said how much she loved them and how sad it was that she could not see them very often, but that she felt they were having a very happy life with their new mummy and daddy.

A few months later she wrote to them again giving her new address, and they haven't shown us the letter or wanted to talk about it.

Our feelings about access are mixed. To be truthful we could live without it, but on the other hand we believe that for the children it has been a good thing. Our children have been, like most other people's, wonderful, fun, maddening, exasperating. Would they have been any different without this access? Maybe so.

Update 1999: The children have continued to meet their birth mother and her two children biannually. It is a happy ending. The contact has been a positive factor in our children's lives. This is in part due to the birth mother's acceptance of the situation and her concern for the children's welfare.

Adopting Charlie

If we had not had open adoption for Charlie I am sure his adoption would have disrupted long ago.

It all started on the day I took Charlie home. I told the social worker that I'd like to meet the birth mother if she agreed. The meeting took place in the social services office, and I was surprised to find that grandma was there too. It was two weeks before Christmas and Charlie was six months old. I was meeting the mother's side of Charlie's family – his father had bolted on learning of his impending fatherhood. The meeting went well and granny told me very firmly that although I was going to be his new mummy, she would always be his granny and he'd always be her grandson. It seemed fitting to promise letters on birthdays and at Christmas.

For two years that was how it was. I just gave basic information and didn't tell her about the problems we were having until it reached the point where I felt I should and that she might be able to help. From then on I just wished that I had been more honest from the beginning.

Charlie's problems started from birth. He had eczema and a milk allergy, but nobody mentioned these to the birth mother or grandmother. Had they done so they would have discovered that his mother suffered in the same way and had spent the first three months of her life in hospital on a diet of glucose and water. By the time Charlie came to us at nearly six months the damage was done. He was screaming with pain and was constantly being sick.

Through granny we found out about other inherent family traits on the maternal side: food allergies, hyperactivity, autism, chronic nosebleeds and his mother's deep sense of insecurity, which he seems to have inherited. From his father's side he inherited his sometimes overwhelming charm but also his behavioural problems: dad, we discovered, had been in a remand home at the age of 14 and was totally irresponsible.

Granny has in a way helped to hold the adoption together. We have regular phone calls and I know that I can call her at any time if I need help or information. His grandmother and mother write to him and I hope the contact will continue.

Charlie takes after both his parents very strongly, totally confounding the social workers' claims that it is nurture rather than nature that counts. Through this open adoption I have been able to prove that Charlie is the way he is because that is the way his birth family is, and that's him. They all tried to blame me and even suggested I should give him up. Without granny's help I might have begun to believe them. Open adoption has worked well for Charlie and us and I'd say to anyone that if the circumstances are right, keep an open avenue.

CHAPTER 11

Adopted but Unattached

Bonding is one of the most fundamental needs between parents and their children, whether those children are 'home-grown' or come into the family through adoption. It is essential to be attached and form intimate bonds with those you live with. Without mutual bonding and learning to trust and love, a child cannot grow the emotional roots he or she needs to develop his or her full potential as an individual.

Adoptive parents are usually well aware of the efforts they have to make to gain a child's trust. But sometimes a child's ability to bond and trust is so damaged by their previous experiences that they are unable to respond to the most loving and sincere of parents, and instead do everything they can to resist loving relationships and remain alone, outside the family unit.

'All adoptees can expect to experience some problems with attachment issues at some time in their lives, but the patterns of behaviour and degree of severity of problems vary dramatically,' says adoptive mother Caroline Archer, a founder of the After Adoption Network within Adoption UK.

At its most extreme this attachment problem requires professional help and has been clinically recognised as Attachment Disorder – a severe emotional problem with long-lasting effects resulting from gross deprivation or abusive parenting. Some adopted children fall into this category. Many other adoptees suffer less severe attachment problems, though even in these cases their ability to make and maintain close relationships may still be affected.

Attachment difficulties can be seen in all types of children, from the tiny baby that stiffens when it is picked up and fails to respond to its parents' nurturing overtures to the teenager who rejects every attempt at love and wilfully turns anything positive into a negative, destructively shaking his or her family to the roots.

Attachment Disorder can be, but is not always, related to genetic make-up. Parents who adopt a sibling group may find that one or two of the children develop healthy attachments but that a third is so traumatised by their early experiences that they are unable to do so. Each child is unique and each child's experience of family life is unique. 'Whilst one child may have received just enough love to get by within the birth family, another will have experienced inconsistency or rejection to such a degree that they cannot trust a parent's love again,' said Caroline Archer.

'This severe lack of trust does not just mean that the child will "test out" their adoptive parents during a "settling in" period: they may persist indefinitely in attempting to prove what they believe deep down – that they are unloveable. A child with distorted attachments disturbs the whole family and both parents and children need professional support over an extended period.'

One frequent symptom of attachment problems is that a child will appear like an angel to outsiders, including the unwary social worker or therapist, whilst causing chaos in their family. The parents then not only have to cope with a troubled child but also with people who feel that 'this lovely child needs rescuing from these angry uptight parents', as one adoptive mother put it.

Another adoptive parent of a child with Attachment Disorder describes her daughter as 'an emotional Sleeping Beauty' who has built up a dense hedge of guarding thorns around herself.

A third parent described herself as 'the mother from hell'. Her personal self-esteem is given a daily bashing not only by her unattached child but also by teachers, friends and peers who question her parenting skills – despite the fact that she has brought up several other children to be well-adjusted, responsible, caring, trusting adults.

A strong sense of personal identity, confidence, rock-firm personal relationships and a bizarre sense of humour are some of the prerequisites for adoptive parents dealing with attachment problems within the family.

Children with attachment problems need to be approached calmly, and parents need to know that the anger they see in their child is not due to them but to significant figures from the child's past. These adoptive parents need professional help which recognises the vital role parents can play in dealing with this problem.

'They need to search for a way to unlock the door to that child's trust,' said one experienced adopter. 'That key can be different for every child.'

● ● ●

Caring for this child can seriously damage your health

Ben was born by Caesarean section, was premature and needed special care. On leaving hospital he spent his next two years in numerous homes with various levels of care, with and without his mother. Following the death of her own mother, Ben's mother reluctantly offered her child for adoption and we were chosen to be his new parents.

As our love for Ben began to develop it became apparent that bringing up this child was going to be different (and difficult). We had never come across a child like him before. We had taken on a whole packet of hurts and rejections, and an inability to trust, to make friends or to love – even himself. At an early stage, when Ben had needed the physical and emotional closeness of his mother, he had not, through circumstances beyond her control, received this precious and special attention. This had left a huge gap in his life which nothing seemed able to fill.

Right from the start, any discipline seemed impossible. He seemed to be saying, 'I have been so hurt in the past that never again could anyone ever hurt me – so do your worst.' No amount of hurt or love was ever going to break the iron walls which surrounded him.

As he grew up there was a continual chain of reports about his behaviour. School found him difficult and he was always in trouble. Experienced staff were manipulated and found themselves being made fools of. A very experienced infant teacher commented that Ben didn't appear to have any conscience.

He couldn't sustain membership at Cubs and other clubs, and we were often taken aside by teaching staff and leaders suggesting that perhaps we were a little too strict and that if we eased up on discipline perhaps he would be less resistant. Yet we knew this child could not function without firm boundaries, and when we were not in sight to remind him of his security and these boundaries he could not cope.

As the years went by we also had to deal with stealing, violence, verbal abuse, lies, deception and denials, together with a desire to spoil or destroy every relationship, toy, book, game, family (or school) event, outing or holiday.

Help was sought from specialised agencies but very little was offered which brought any significant change. Everything we knew in our hearts to be right was questioned. This child needed firm boundaries and there was no shortage of love.

On referral to psychologists, family therapists and psychiatrists we came away feeling that we had been exaggerating about his behaviour, as when talking with Ben they seemed to find him most charming and articulate. When asked how we handled particular situations we felt we were offering 'textbook' answers, and because they did not appear to be working the professionals seemed to think we were lying! It was apparent that most parents brought up their children by instinct – why then was this not working for us? It had in the past. Why did professionals, clergy, family and friends doubt that our instincts were as good as theirs? Why did nobody understand our situation?

We knew we were not 'fighting' flesh and blood and Ben had said on some occasions, from quite an early age, 'It's not me doing these things – it's something I cannot control from inside.'

Some friends from a local church heard about the problems we were experiencing and invited us to their home, offering to pray with Ben and us. One of them had been adopted and she seemed to understand immediately how we were all feeling. First, they asked Ben to tell them how he felt about what he had been doing and suggested that it was not the real Ben who had been behaving in that way. They explained that he could be rid of all these things that made him unhappy such as his anger and stealing.

They prayed together, requesting the spirit of anger to leave Ben. Ben said that he could see Satan in a flowing black cloak go crashing to his death to the bottom of a deep valley, and there he was, all smashed to pieces. I commented that he had been reading too many comics but Ben said, 'No Mum, this is for real.' Ben said his inside felt like the emptying of bath water. Finally, they prayed for the Holy Spirit to fill Ben and to fill all the empty spaces left by the bad spirits.

Afterwards, Ben chose to snuggle into his dad's arms and lay there peacefully – those with experience of children with Attachment Disorder will know how unusual (and wonderful) that was.

The whole experience was like witnessing a rebirth, a new creation, so we can only say, 'Thank you, God.'

Five years have passed and none of us will ever forget that occasion. Ben still refers to it and asks for prayer whenever things get tough. He soon resumed mainstream education, still has ups and downs, but any difficult behaviour is a shadow of the past. It is as though from that moment on, that part within him that had been unreachable – the part which could not feel love, the part which could only respond with anger – began to melt away, and in its place trust and love is growing. He wants to please, to love and to be loved. His personality has not changed: he has a wonderful sense of humour, can talk the hind leg off a donkey, is still untidy and loses everything that is not attached. But he put his arm around me the other day and said, 'Thanks, Mum, for sticking by me', and he meant it.

Attached and unattached – age isn't the issue

Luke was four when he was placed for adoption. He had been in care from the age of two weeks and social services, health authority workers, the police and the NSPCC had all been very concerned about his condition. His birth mother was 18. She was homeless and lived with Luke in numerous bed and breakfast hotels, and there were frequent changes of partner. She suffered from depression and was unable to care for him. Luke suffered serious neglect, both physical and emotional, and was put on the abuse register after an incident with one of the boyfriends.

He was taken to foster parents at the age of two and a half when his sister Natasha was born. He remained with the foster parents until he came to us aged four. Luke's social worker was marvellous. Luke saw him as a friend – he was supportive and able to help him to understand all the changes through skilled use of play therapy. I'm convinced this helped his future development enormously.

Luke is now approaching his teens and is a real joy to have around. He understands fully about being adopted and feels relaxed enough to talk about it when he wants to. He is close to us and so rewarding, and has coped brilliantly with all the problems he has suffered in his life.

We applied to adopt a younger child as a sister or brother for Luke. During the assessment we were told about Natasha and Jamie (Luke's real sister and brother, who were born after he was taken into care and who were now in care themselves). We thought it would be great to keep them together with their elder brother. They were placed with us when Luke was six. Natasha was three and Jamie a lively toddler.

Things were rather tough at first but we were confident that everything would fall into place. Natasha in particular was very confused by the whole thing and, with limited speech, was unable to articulate her worries. Jamie was able to cope with the changes and has developed from a lively toddler into a lively seven-year-old. He is very bright – hard work for his teacher – loving and super company.

From very early on it was clear to us (though not to anyone else) that Natasha was having severe problems relating to us. Through intuition and experience I felt our concerns were justified. However, I was gradually beaten down into feeling it was all my fault and that it was a 'personality clash'. I was 'too analytical' or simply 'exaggerating'. Nobody understood. This little girl was charming, intelligent and articulate with strangers and could keep up this act for days while grandparents stayed. With us she was disruptive, sullen and moody, opting out of the family as fast as possible, and yet refusing to give us any peace by constantly winding us all up. Natasha put an increasing strain on all the relationships within the family.

After six long years, a friend heard about Reactive Attachment Disorder and recognised Natasha's problems in what was being discussed. We sent for the Adoption UK resource pack for parents and felt as though a great weight had been lifted off our shoulders. We have been so helped by Adoption UK and other parents of RAD children.

In desperation for some kind of help for Natasha and for us, we have asked for social services involvement. This was a big step for us and time will tell whether it was the right one. The workers assigned to our case seem to listen and understand, and they have a good theoretical understanding of the condition. We have met with them several times and Natasha could win an Oscar for her charming and utterly convincing performance. She is astonishing.

At the present time it could go either way. Perhaps the social workers will hang on to the information we've given them and appreciate that there is another side to Natasha that they may never see but will have to take our word for – or they may be totally charmed by her and once again she'll avoid being challenged and thus avoid being helped. Alarm bells are sounding in my head and I already sense that they are questioning our approach.

One positive thing has come out of our meeting: this sad, furious child who claims that she doesn't love any of us and wants to live with someone else has scared herself by making that statement to a social worker and is now back-pedalling like mad to ensure her place with us and reassure herself that we do love her. If we can hold on to her (in every sense) perhaps we'll get through in the end.

The milder end of Attachment Disorder

After reading about Attachment Disorder I felt that most of the problems I had with my children were so mild they weren't worth talking about. But bringing up a child with only a low level of Attachment Disorder can be incredibly frustrating.

Children with any attachment difficulties seem somehow able to recruit all sorts of people to their cause. As a parent you find yourself cast in the role of ogre while your child snuggles up shamelessly to neighbours, friends and visiting aunties, who invariably say something like, 'Oh, the poor little soul. Surely she can have another biscuit…sweetie…stay up a little later…', without the slightest idea that this trifling issue is in fact a battle area in which you, as parent, need to be victorious. With such apparently little things, it seems so petty to say no, but it's the hidden agenda that only child and parent recognise that's in operation at times like this.

Our daughter was only a baby when she came to us and she began as she meant to go on. When we met her she looked steadily at me, turned away almost dismissively and gave my husband a huge grin. A collective wave of 'Ahs' went round the assembled audience, my husband was overwhelmed and I knew I hadn't a hope – even though I had been made distinctly uneasy by my first eye contact with that scheming little lady! Now, at 22, she has the guts and the self-understanding to admit that her first concern with any new relationship was always: 'What's in it for me?' I had an extremely tough time bringing her up, but I love and admire her. She still exasperates me. She still tends to lurch from one disaster to another in her personal life. I still have to protect other members of the family against her excesses at times. I still wonder if anything in my life, particularly my bank account, will ever be truly mine. But she is my daughter and I love her, and the bond that has eventually grown between us is worth all the pain and tears.

With no biological bond in place, I had to work hard to create an emotional one, to let this small person know that I was her mother and the person in charge of her daily life. Even as a baby, she acted as though she was desperate to be in charge of her own affairs. I felt very strongly that her short experience of life had left her feeling that there was no one to look out for her but herself: she had been let down and, therefore, it was up to her to sort out her own affairs. If she could have changed her own nappies and made her own bottles she would have done it.

Schoolteachers, from nursery to comprehensive school, invariably started their acquaintances with her cooing delightedly over her beauty, her sweetness and her overall 'cuteness'. Within weeks they would be tearing their hair out and usually maligning me and my child-rearing methods (in spite of the fact that our older children had passed through their hands as well and had given no trouble). I've been told that I didn't love my daughter enough and that I loved her too much for her own good; that I hadn't given her enough discipline and that I gave her too much. Maybe if she'd been my first child I would have cracked up completely. As it was, my self-esteem took an enormous hammering and I experienced shattering doubts about my own ability to parent. I began to think my experience with my older children had just been good luck.

But we survived the difficult years and I firmly believe that certain factors helped. These included a strong marital relationship in which we worked together as a team and trusted one another completely. Having other children who appeared to be well adjusted, happy and mature helped us to realise that we were getting some things right, and probably saved our sanity! We also had interests and activities outside the home which gave us opportunities to think about other things.

So many parents of children with Attachment Disorder seem to feel the same sense of shame that battered wives feel. We have to reaffirm to ourselves that although our children's behaviour is not their fault, it isn't our fault either.

Update 1999: In the four years since writing this our daughter has married and had two small daughters of her own. She is a fantastic mother, and we are all very proud of her.

Bonding doesn't just happen

We visited Andrew at his foster home for four days prior to bringing him home. I was so excited, yet scared and apprehensive. Andrew was five months old. He had been with his birth mother for two days and then with his foster parents, where he had stayed until he came to us.

We had the baby we had so longed for. I was quite overwhelmed by the whole experience. It was not how I had imagined it would be, which made me feel guilt. Love was not instant – it took a while to grow. He was sometimes a difficult baby to love because he was not cuddly at all and was often very serious, although he ate and slept really well and seemed contented. I thought he would become more cuddly after a while but this didn't happen. I felt that something was not quite right. Andrew used to wriggle in my arms and would never sit still, even as a small baby. You just couldn't cuddle him, even when he was in distress.

At his eight-month check, when the doctor asked if I had any worries, I told her about his rejecting behaviour. She felt that in time this would pass, as he was probably still getting used to us. I felt relieved and hoped things would improve, but they didn't. Something was wrong. He was not at all friendly with strangers (a problem that is linked with Attachment Disorder in fact); he was quite the reverse.

I started reading articles about the symptoms of Attachment Disorder and began to think that maybe this was the problem, though I found it strange that such a straightforward adoption could cause AD. But the more I read the more convinced I became. I was sent lots of literature which included bonding techniques and I found this very useful.

I feel angry that nobody mentioned the possibility of AD to me or even that bonding doesn't just happen and that there are things you should do as soon as your child comes home with you. About a year after adopting Andrew his rejecting behaviour began to be targeted at me and not my husband, who was always the 'goody' whilst I was cast in the role of the 'baddy'.

I contacted my doctor when Andrew was about 13 months old and she referred us to a psychologist. She feels that Andrew may have a mild form of autism, which should not really affect him as he grows older, that it may be part of his personality or that it may be Attachment Disorder, which she admits to knowing very little about. She has said Andrew is an unusual child but does not want to label him at the tender age of two.

We also contacted our social worker. He was surprised to hear of our problems and came to see us. He felt there was nothing wrong and that maybe it was we who were expecting too much of Andrew. No further visit or support was offered. We felt let down, angry and even began to wonder if we were doing something wrong. The only helpful advice came from the After Adoption Network within Adoption UK. We still have a long way to go but some things we have tried have improved him.

- Eye contact is much better now. We sing to him, talk to him with lots of enthusiasm and hold him in positions in which he does have to look at us.

- We share as many things as we can and have fun together.

- His acceptance of tickling and touching has improved as a result of us doing it often, but he does not enjoy it for long.

- Andrew will sit on our laps now for quite some time, reading, watching TV together and sharing what's going on.

- We bath together.

- We work to keep his attention with lots of enthusiasm and fun.

- We get kisses and cuddles now, but have to ask for them.

- We make things reciprocal wherever possible.

Time has made the bonding improve and he is much more trusting of us now, as though a bit of his barrier has come down.

Update 1999: We went to do some holding therapy and this has been particularly beneficial. Our relationship has improved tremendously. Our son is now much more loving, happier in himself and less 'tantrumy'. After the first couple of sessions, I remember feeling so happy and loved for the first time since he came home with us as a baby. It wasn't easy to hold on while he kicked and pushed to get away but afterwards it all seemed worthwhile.

Candle flame

Our child was placed four years ago and was soon displaying symptoms we now know to be typical of a child with Reactive Attachment Disorder. As time passed life with her became more difficult as she cut herself off from family life, preferring her own fantasy world. It was impossible to have a conversation with her – indeed she ignored me (her mum) totally for more than a year, refusing to speak. Her rejection of me was all-encompassing.

After a respite break, it was suggested that I might try using a lighted candle to help her talk. While the candle is lit, everyone is free to say exactly what they feel and can speak about anything honestly; when the flame is blown out, everything that has been said is gone – there are no repercussions.

Having had no meaningful conversation with my daughter for over two years I was a bit dubious, but decided nonetheless to try. To my amazement, after I had described to her what was to happen, there followed a remarkable outpouring. The candlelight seemed to hold her attention, creating an intimacy in which I was able to soothe, reassure and comfort her and she was able to accept this. I found the experience relaxing and was able to act in a calm and loving way, which had not always been the case in the past. My daughter was able to share where previously she had been unable to. Focusing on the flame, she seemed subconsciously to be able to accept the comfort which would have been rejected before. Her relief was tangible when she was able to blow out the flame, but the closeness between us remained.

We have used the technique on several occasions and each time has been a breakthrough. It may have been that she was in a particularly vulnerable state and was ready to accept our help at last, but it has certainly had positive results in our family.

The mother from hell

I am the parent of a teenage boy with 'a few problems'. Scanning a list of Reactive Attachment Disorder symptoms I realise this is a description of my child.

We as parents must now come to terms with the reality that we and our child, adopted at four and not 14, are not fully bonded.

We are bewildered but caring parents stuck in a perpetual 'terrible twos' phase and heading straight for awful adolescence. One adopter we know confessed that her teenager turned, almost overnight, into the 'daughter from hell'. The damage done to parents over the years must eventually become apparent.

My child was suspended from school (for the hundredth time, or so it seemed) for quite a serious misdemeanour. Mum and dad drop everything, race up to the school, do battle with the enemy (headteacher, psychologist, etc.), come home, sit down and have deep and meaningful discussions about what went wrong this time. I feel strangely close to my son at this point. I see his vulnerability and need. We plan a quiet day at home.

The next day dawns, his room's a mess as always and I go spare! Ranting and raving, I threaten all sorts of punishments. Both he and I know that he is not being raved at for a messy room but for the humiliation, embarrassment and upset of yesterday, which we all coped with so well, didn't we? But did we? What did I say about the daughter from hell? Try mother instead.

But help is at hand. Support groups are emerging. The old well-worn philosophy of talking with people who have had similar experiences, this giving and getting of support and strength, has kept many adopters who have been in despair sane.

The mother from hell waits patiently and with hope.

Eight-year-old teenager

At the moment we are totally frustrated and angry at having to go round and round in ever-decreasing circles coping with an eight-year-old teenager who lacks personal esteem, hates school and herself and constantly believes that she is unlovely and therefore unloved. I believe that the counselling both she and we are receiving, however well intentioned and delivered, is like trying to cure cancer with an aspirin. It cannot get through the subconscious defence mechanisms that our daughter has developed in order to pretend there is nothing wrong. It leaves her unable to mature emotionally, and this is a bleak future for all of us.

Christmas with ADHD

Our son Alan is 14 and has ADHD (Attention Deficit Hyperactivity Disorder), ODD (Oppositional Defiance Disorder) and dyslexia, none very severely. We get compliments from friends about his behaviour when we are at their homes, but at our house and out and about he can be very trying. Because his condition is home-centred he has never caused any real trouble at school and he is popular with his peers of both sexes, so he hasn't suffered from social isolation. He is just hell on wheels at home. This is a diary of our Christmas holiday.

Saturday. He was fiddling with a watch he had found on the street and had taken it to pieces. The girls came to tell me that he was crying because he had broken it. I went to him and he was crying. It took me ages to work out that he was crying because he wanted to be with his birth family, and not because of the watch at all.

That evening my wife and I were invited to a party without the kids. We managed to rope my 81-year-old mother into babysitting for the children. Alan declared that he was going over the road to his friend's for the evening. We agreed with the provision that bedtime was still ten o'clock. We got home at twelve-thirty to find granny asleep but distraught when we woke her up. Alan was gone. At ten-past-ten she had phoned the friend's house to find that Alan had gone out. I took her home. Before going out to scour the highways and byways I decided to check Alan's bedroom, and there he was, sound asleep. He had done this before: come home late and sneaked upstairs to avoid a row.

Sunday passed off without serious incident. In fact, at morning chapel I glowed with pride as I watched him set up the amplifiers for the band.

Christmas morning. He complains about his presents, trying to flog off the less favoured items to his parents and siblings. His own presents to people consisted entirely of sweets and chocolates, bought in five minutes as cheaply as possible, whereas the other children had spent more money and taken time to consider what they gave. We are not a materialistic family, much to our son's disgust, but we try to stress choosing thoughtfully even though there is not much to spend. Time to go to chapel. I went to scrape the ice off the car window. He and two friends were larking around and I gave him the keys to turn on the radio, start the heater, etc. But he decided to go for a spin. We park in a municipal car park. It was covered in ice, and there he was driving and sliding around with his friends in the back. We banned him from seeing the friends for two days, and it will be some time before he gets his hands on the car keys again, although at six feet tall there is probably not a lot I could do physically to stop him now. He was extremely surly at Christmas dinner at his grandmother's and I had to take him home early to ease the strain on the rest of the family.

During *Hook* on TV I sat in the middle of the sofa with him on one side. Then our youngest started hysterics because she wanted to sit by me. Alan left the room. He returned after an hour in a very bad temper, yelling at everyone. Eventually, I made him leave the room and he stomped upstairs. I followed after ten minutes to find him in tears again, clutching a carved pendant his birth parents had given him when we visited them. I think this is the hardest thing about open adoption at this age. I was soon in tears too because there is practically nothing we can do to alleviate the pain.

On Boxing Day evening we had a party for four families. It started out fine, but Alan gradually became more and more excited and eventually had to be physically restrained from throwing the contents of his brother's bedroom out of the second floor window.

The next day I managed to stop him just in time, before he began to flood the path with water so it would freeze overnight to make a skating rink.

December 30. I caught Alan with a hammer and chisel trying to chip the ice off the garden path. I had told him two days ago not to do that but he couldn't remember.

New Year's Eve. This was our older daughter's tenth birthday party. To our surprise Alan behaved fine at another party which lasted until one in the morning.

CHAPTER 12

The Nightmare

When an Adoption Breaks Down

It's a nightmare scenario – the thought of a child that you have nurtured going back into institutionalised care or being taken from your arms to be returned to birth parents who have unexpectedly changed their minds. It happens.

Like all tragedies, it happens for a number of different reasons. There might be an unrecognised problem that doesn't go away as everyone thought it might but grows until it becomes unbearable. It could be as simple and devastating as a birth mother suddenly changing her mind about placing her baby for adoption. It can be as complicated as an adoptive parent asking for a little respite from the child they love but find difficult to live with, and finding that instead of receiving support they are judged to be unable to cope and the child is removed permanently.

Others find that try as they might – sometimes over many years – the child they have tried to include in their family just doesn't want to be a part of it. Sometimes adoptees have such deep-rooted problems as a result of their past that they are unable to make relationships or be a part of a family.

Society makes its own judgements of adoptive parents who are having problems with an adopted child. The adopter often finds a lack of sympathy from their peers – after all, they have 'chosen' this child. It's an unfair 'you've made your bed and you must lie in it' approach. And the misery felt by adopters when things go wrong is often deemed to be less valid than that of parents facing similar problems with children born to them.

Even some social workers appear to criticise rather than support the adoptive parent. Although they will do everything in their power to return or keep a child with his or her birth family, the same rules don't seem to apply to adoptive families.

One adoptive mother traumatised by the breakdown of a placement said: 'My first advice to other adoptive parents in the same situation might be: avoid the social services if at all possible, they operate with a "blaming" model rather than a "helping" model when it comes to childcare cases.'

'It's a strange thing, this adoption business. When things go wrong you can feel very isolated as an adoptive parent and that isolation doesn't help the situation at all,' said another adopter.

As when anything else in life goes badly wrong, days, months and even years are filled with regrets. Here are some very different tales of broken hearts.

● ● ●

Adoption story

Even now when everything is chill
I hear our thrill.
They've chosen Us.
Our own, if still another's.
They posed you
like an old time
waif and stray
hunched up against a doorway,
closed up, hugged in,
staring at the camera.
Hard eyes, clenched grin,
'giving nowt away'.

You passed the photo test.
They hung a placard
round your neck,
begging Be My Parent.
But you'd already second-guessed
the double dare in that.
The other words told even less:
healthy and boisterous,
seven-year-old,
lively, energetic,
bit of a scold,
needs lots of love and
to be told:
'You're here to stay.'

We met you in the Home
from home, the aunties smiled,
the kids looked sour,
we played Happy Families
for an hour, then took you
to the park, played hide and seek
and tried to lark about.
You kept your distance,
shrugged away the bribes,
we hunted cows, and sheep,
to keep alive the hopes
we'd piggybacked on your revival.

Once 'settled in' your questions
were always whats and ifs

what would you do if
this bridge blew up?
Our house burnt down?
The lollipop man
(who looked like Freddy)
went for us with a Coca-Cola can?
Round every corner
little Jack Horner
was waiting with a battering ram.

The family album shows one side,
the trips, the treats,
the funfair rides, smiling poses,
cheek by jowl, rough and tumble,
playful growls, while out of focus,
out of reach, the baby bandit
stalked the beach,
thumb in mouth and fist in air
each rasp of rage
a wordless gesture at despair.

'These strangers came from faraway
and took me home with them.
They were kind but old.
I liked the flat and cats.
I wanted a good cooker lady
and a dad who's strong.
I got a painter with a woolly hat
and a man who lived for books and chat.
They wanted a brainy head,
they got a ragamuffin
with street cred instead.
They made me see a therapist,
she asked me lots about my mum
and then got personal.
I never asked for all this stuff.
Enough's enough.'

Our name went first,
then things,
moving to a smaller room,
bare walls,
back Home at last.
No strings.
Not just the usual casting off;

these toys and clothes
were not outgrown
but never grown into.
The love they meant
too much to bear
because it also spoke of loss
of what and who
was never there.

New furies
turned attrition
into open war,
your body changed,
your anger grew.
'You took me from my mum.
You're shit.'
We hit back
with the 'Care Bear' script.

Punch-drunk,
we slugged it out,
growing desperate
to stop the rout
of all our best intentions.
Too late:
we were too mirrored
in your hate
to open any other door
than one marked exit.

We meet again on neutral ground.
He sits hunched in the chair
closed up, hugged in,
staring at the one-way mirror,
hard eyes, clenched grin,
giving nowt away.
An old hand
at this game,
the social worker turns to us
and says, 'Now tell me,
how did it all begin?'

By Phil Cohen

Our nearly daughter

As a young couple, naive in the ways of adoption, we had a two-month-old baby placed with us. We brought her home on Christmas Eve – the most wonderful present we had ever had. Two months later came an unexpected visit from our social worker, who said: 'I'm sorry, the mother's changed her mind. She wants her baby back.' This was many years ago. We have adopted since, and have a lovely family. I could never say we 'got over' the experience of losing our daughter, but we got used to it.

I can think more rationally now about that baby's birth mother and how she must have felt. Ironically enough, she and her husband were a couple experiencing difficulty in conceiving. After a short separation and reunion, the young wife realised she was pregnant by a man with whom she had a brief liaison during the separation from her husband. What a dilemma this pregnancy must have been. For the husband, the knowledge that his wife could conceive with someone else; for the wife, the dread that this baby, possibly the only one she would bear, would have to be given up to save her marriage. They might, in other circumstances, have chosen to present the baby as a child of the marriage and keep the truth to themselves – but this choice wasn't theirs. They were white: the baby's birth father was black.

I found it difficult in the middle of our own heartbreak to feel compassion for the baby's family. I understood their anguish in the reasonable part of myself, but in my heart I felt only pain and anger. I too felt 'used'. There was a strong suspicion that the social workers had pushed through an adoption placement in order to bring the mother to her senses. She had, according to them, been ready to leave the child in foster care, staying in touch with the baby's father while living with her husband, and playing off one man against the other. I am sure now that she was so desperate to keep her child that she was trying to preserve all options. She might have chosen either man had they helped her to keep the baby.

When the baby left us she went to her maternal grandparents, but I found out a year or so later that she eventually made her home with her mother and her mother's husband. I don't know how much guilt, blame and reconciliation surrounded this child, but I hope so much that the family survived and stayed together.

What I wonder now is whether the child, when she is old enough, will discover anything about her early history. She will know from her own appearance that her father is not her birth father. She was baptised while she was with us – with her birth name, since she was not adopted – but her baptismal entry will show a ceremony in a church some miles from her home, with godparents she will never have heard of. Our names do not appear, since we were not her parents. The family friends who stood as godparents are aware of the very slight possibility that she will find them and would, I know, receive her warmly and wisely. But will her parents ever explain the riddle of her baptism, or will they keep the evidence hidden from her? She will not approach the adoption agency for an explanation since she is not adopted, and probably doesn't know that this was ever planned.

Our children know about their 'nearly sister' (we didn't remove her photos from the family album) and they have always been quite intrigued by the thought of her. We cannot look forward to any reunion. We are not her birth parents. We are nothing to her at all, although she will always remain part of our lives – our 'nearly daughter'.

When things don't work out

Adrian was described as 'a friendly, outgoing boy who got on well with adults and children alike'. In our naivety we believed this assessment of him by his social worker. Laura, his sister, was younger and eagerly awaiting a new family.

After a very protracted introduction they moved in. Laura loved it from the first day. She mixed well in her new school and made friends. She responded well to a new routine and was delighted with treats, her new family, new food, everything!

Adrian was more reserved, less able to let go. He seemed less committed. We put this down to him being older and having different experiences. He had been in care before; Laura had lived with their birth mother until six months before she came to live with us.

It wasn't long before we realised that Adrian valued material things above all else. We thought we could cope with this by explaining about time and thought behind a gift, and so on. He told lies and stole long before we ever found out about it. When confronted with a problem he would be silent, adding to our frustration. Academically he was well above average, and an endless stream of teachers reported how difficult it was to keep him occupied. His work was usually done carelessly and in a hurry, and when finished he would disrupt the class.

Adrian manipulated people. He knew to be on his best behaviour with grandparents and our friends. This made it difficult to explain what we were experiencing. Almost everything became a battleground and family life was very strained.

We learned that the birth family had been in family therapy before Adrian and Laura came into care. It was thought that it might help if we went now. We did, and it didn't. We (without the children) saw a psychologist, and that helped a little, but we realised that we were learning to live with his behaviour. No one was helping Adrian to live with his experiences.

Finally, the decision for Adrian to leave was made. He had been asking to leave and for all our sakes it was the only solution to a problem that was eating into all of us. For over three years we had tried to make it work. His leaving was sad but also a release. The tension left and Laura matured. Her adoption was straightforward and a joy.

Three years on Adrian is with a foster family, his fourth placement since leaving us. He spent a short time with his birth mother, but this eventually broke down. Adrian rings Laura each time he moves. Laura chats but is not interested in maintaining a regular relationship.

We have never regretted making the decision that Adrian should leave. We had to hold on to what was good, and not sacrifice Laura and ourselves for Adrian. Of course there were 'if onlys' and 'we could haves', but we did the best we could. We were not the family for Adrian.

Very little, if any, preparation work for moving to a new family had been done with the children. Their individual needs had not been looked at and no consideration had been given to the question of whether they should be placed together. We had not been given the full details of their past. When challenged about the behaviour Adrian had displayed that led to family therapy the social worker said that he didn't feel we needed to know!

The above paragraph contains all the ingredients for the breakdown of a placement. However, Laura's placement is a complete success. Perhaps Laura was lucky and Adrian was not – but should luck really play such a major part in the adoption process?

If we accept, as we must, that not every relationship works out, whether it be within marriage, the workplace or the extended family, then we must accept that some adoption placements will not work either. Therefore, we must ensure that commitment, honesty and realism are present in every person at every point in the adoption process. Only then will the risk of disruption, with its attendant pain, rejection, guilt and sense of loss, be kept to a minimum.

Don't give up

Michael came to us on a fostering basis at the age of six. There were no particular problems with adoption and when he was seven he became our son legally. We were aware that Michael could develop severe psychological problems as a result of emotional and physical deprivations, but we thought we could cope and went ahead with the adoption in good faith.

Inevitably, Michael underachieved at school, but he made some progress. However, his constant nightmares, enuresis and the difficulty he had in coping with close family relationships all indicated underlying emotional stress. He loved his little sister when she came to us at three months old, but gradually he began to feel threatened by her, and lying and stealing together with unacceptable domestic behaviour became part of the scene. Unexpectedly, when Michael was 14 and his sister five, we had a child of our own, and although we tried desperately to convey to Michael that our care and concern for him were undiminished, things went from bad to worse and his aggressive, threatening behaviour totally disrupted family life.

We had some support from one social worker by this time who, unfortunately, only alienated Michael completely. We tried family therapy, but this was unsympathetically conducted and was counter-productive, Michael being the first to say how useless it was. It was suggested that we try holding therapy, but Michael was by then so big and strong that we felt it was not right for us. Next, he attended a residential unit for disturbed children during the week and came home at weekends. The peace of those weeks without him made us see even more clearly how abnormal life had become.

To cut a long story short, we felt we could not survive as a family in these circumstances. We had two other children to consider, so Michael was taken back into care, and although it was the hardest decision we ever had to make the relief of knowing that we were no longer responsible for him or his behaviour was enormous. It enabled us to start afresh and it enabled Michael to escape from the relationships that he was finding so impossible to deal with at home. After a relatively settled period in a residential and caring community, he got into trouble with the police and was sent to a remand centre for six months when he was 18.

During these difficult years we felt terribly guilty that we were not able to cope better with Michael. It was hard even to make the initial approach to social services, as somehow that seemed to be admitting defeat. When we adopted Michael there had been no question of ongoing support in spite of the difficulties forecast – but, oh, how we would have rejoiced had it been available. Each day that Michael was at home became a nightmare, and we were so obsessed with Michael and his problems that we could think and talk of little else – in spite of our joy in our small daughter and baby son.

However, this is not the end of the story. Being on remand gave Michael time to think, and when he came out he was clearly determined to make something of his life. Since then, as the years have gone by, he has had his lucky breaks and his setbacks, has formed a steady relationship with his girlfriend, with whom he is now living, and has set up his own small business. We had never completely lost touch, even in the most difficult times, and now he visits us regularly and clearly appreciates his family.

I suppose the moral to this story is that it is worth holding on to a relationship, however tenuously. Going back into care does not have to sever relationships completely. Michael has determination and charm, and but for his strength of character he would not have surmounted his difficulties as he has done. All credit to him for living in the present and the future and for not blaming the past for his misfortunes.

PS: Michael, now aged 22, after reading the above, added these further points. Children are not accountable for their own actions. They hit out at the nearest thing, which is not necessarily the cause of their aggression. Don't give up on your children, whatever happens.

Update 1999: Two and a quarter years ago Michael committed suicide at the age of 27. It is hard to appreciate the fragility and vulnerability of children badly damaged in their early years. Those of us who were brought up in a secure and loving environment can have no real conception of the inner confusions and tortured emotions that arise as these children become adults and have to face up to the real world, with its responsibilities and relationships.

Michael had married, had three children, and his business was doing well. But then he became involved in an unfortunate miscarriage of justice, with which he became obsessed. In his efforts to maintain control of where his life was going he had become domineering and abusive in his treatment of his wife and eldest child (who was his stepchild). Eventually, their relationships became so bad that his wife threatened to leave him. He suddenly became aware of all that he stood to lose and tried desperately to put things right. But when it became apparent that the marriage was really not going to work, his emotional reserves were by this time so low and his feelings of loss and rejection so great that he felt that the only way out was to take his own life.

I write this sequel because the story is incomplete without it. I also write it because I want the world to know the measure of the hurt and pain these children endure. I want the world to know how essential it is that they have good counselling and/or therapy as early as possible and for as long and as often as is needed. I want the world to know how desperately the adoptive parents of these damaged children need support. I want people to understand that we grieve because the love we gave him was not enough, and feel immensely sad at his death, but also that we feel proud that he achieved so much given such terrible emotional wounds. Despite all the difficulties and traumas, there were many moments of shared happiness, and his years with us added immeasurably to the richness of our lives.

The nightmare: Adopted children going back into care

For most adoptive parents the very idea of their chosen child going back into care (and what a misnomer that is!) is unthinkable. After years of struggling with sometimes difficult and disturbed children, some of us find that the response to requests for help is to institute care proceedings. I write this whilst still traumatised by one such experience.

I have three adopted children, very widely spaced – a son now 20, a daughter just 15 and a young son aged seven. I have never regretted adopting my two sons, although neither of them has been problem-free. The main thing is that we bonded, and they have both given me a great deal of joy and happiness. With my daughter this never seemed to happen, although when she was younger I was always trying to persuade myself that we were on the verge of a breakthrough.

My daughter is an unbonded or unattached child, despite all my efforts. One symptom of this was the way she dominated and controlled us all whilst being resistant to normal parental control. Another was the way in which she drew outsiders into family affairs by bestowing affection widely and promiscuously whilst holding back from us, by 'telling' strangers about her early life and by inventing and embroidering stories about family members. All of this was very sad and betrayed that she was a child desperately in need of love but unable to receive it, to whom the satisfaction of wielding power seemed a substitute for being loved.

As she got older all these behaviours became worse and she discovered the dramatic effect of making allegations about us in public.

I sought help far and wide but none appeared to address the problem or make any difference, and by the time I got to social services I was in despair. I had little choice but to approach them, for my daughter had by then (aged just 12) turned violent and was going missing from home until late at night.

Over the next two years I fought hard for proper supervision for my daughter and help for the family. We asked for a brief period of respite, then for therapy, then for special schooling as she was effectively excluded from three schools in succession. All of this was either refused or failed to be provided. As matters got worse at home (we were living in a state of siege) my daughter eventually had to go into voluntary care (what they now call 'accommodation') – at first in a foster home, and then when this broke down, in a children's home.

By the time I won my battle for special schooling my daughter was out of everyone's control. A horrific incident when she was abducted and beaten up by strangers finally led social services to agree to an out-of-authority placement. At last I had peace of mind – she was safe and so were we, and I tried to rebuild some kind of relationship with her. I never lost touch with her, visited and rang her frequently, and had her at home for long visits during this two and a half years. The school turned out to be excellent and the teachers were happy for me to continue contact with my daughter.

It was when she absconded from the school with a much younger girl that social services took a different stance. On absconding she came home and when I tried to inform the police she broke several windows and stalked off. After going missing for two weeks she turned herself in to social services. It was at this point that the new nightmare began. She told them she was not going back to the school – so they didn't send her! She told them that she didn't want to see me – so they instituted care proceedings! Although my daughter was technically 'accommodated' at this point (which means that I retained ultimate parental responsibility and should have been consulted) these decisions were made without consulting me.

When the case came to court four days later the social worker's statement raked up old allegations and implied that there was truth in them. Unbeknownst to me, when I had gone to social services two years earlier for help because my daughter had become physically violent, my daughter had alleged to social workers that I hit her. This was never discussed with me. This now appeared in the statement as the reason for social services involvement. The statement concluded that my daughter's problems were all to be blamed on me, and that contact between us should be limited and subject to their express permission.

Update 1999: The case described above had a happy ending. I won, after 18 months of fighting and numerous postponements of the final hearing. Meanwhile, social services continued to pay for my daughter's special placement and she continued to blow hot and cold, sometimes wanting to see me, sometimes not and frequently disappearing.

Two weeks ago the phone rang. It was my daughter, now nearly 20, singing 'Happy birthday to you' down the line. A week later the phone rang again. It was the police from a nearby town ringing with another message from my daughter: 'Tell me mum I've been arrested.'

This may sound like a bleak tale. My daughter sometimes describes herself as an outcast – though she eagerly grasped the opportunity to be an outsider. I imagine her as a pirate ship in stormy seas – a ship with a very, very long anchor: me.

CHAPTER 13

Telling, Talking and the Need to Know More

Once upon a time, telling meant making sure your child knew before they could talk that they were adopted and just as special as born-to children, but different in that they had another set of genetic birth parents.

But a generation ago, beyond knowing that their birth parents were unable to keep them, an adopted child would be told little about their family of birth – what they did, where they came from or even what they looked like. Today, a full package of good and bad background knowledge appears with a child looking for adoption, whether they are a babe in arms, a gangly-legged schoolgirl or a downy-cheeked teenage boy.

Telling and talking starts on day one of the adoption. 'Telling is something so vital in the growing up of an adopted child that it should not be referred to as "telling" but as "knowing",' said one adoptive mother. She suggests that adoption should be part of the daily dialogue between adoptive parent and child from the first days they are together, even if the child is just a baby. From day one a child needs to know that they are different but that this difference is positive.

For a child adopted at an older age there is no need to tell, but there is a need to talk about the circumstances surrounding their adoption so that they can learn to understand and hopefully come to terms with the past. 'They may have plenty of memories of life before adoption, but as time goes by these will become fainter or will change. Things take on new significance as they grow older. They will want to check out their memories and the importance or reality of events and people they remember or know about, and discuss anew the reasons for people's actions and decisions,' said Patricia Swanton, an adoptive mother. 'Adoption is a lifelong process, and even as an adult an adopted person will often need to look at their adoption from a new viewpoint – for instance, when an adoptee has children of their own.'

'Adoptive children, whatever the circumstances of their birth and adoption, need to be given the opportunity to talk about their birth family. It is a subject they may sometimes feel uncomfortable about raising themselves because they don't want to appear "disloyal". It is up to the adoptive parents to give their children the opportunity to talk,' said one adopter. One obvious opportunity is a child's birthday. 'At the end of a day full of excitement and celebration you can talk about what a special day your child's birth was to his or her mother and how that day would be remembered by them. It is vital that the subject of an adoptee's birth parents is left open for discussion – if and when wanted.'

Without open discussion, an adopted child can feel guilty about the break-up of their birth family, fearing or assuming that it was their fault. They need reassurance that it was not: it is adults who should take responsibility, not children.

And whatever the circumstances of their adoption children must feel positive about their origins. 'Abused and neglected children will have memories that may be sad or painful, but they may also have some good memories. It can be difficult and confusing if they feel both love and anger with their birth parents,' says Patricia Swanton. 'They need help from their adoptive parents and maybe professional help as well in sorting out these feelings and salvaging something positive.' Disabled children have to cope with the worry that had they been born able-bodied their birth parents might not have relinquished them. They need reassurance that they were loved but that their birth parents were anxious that they wouldn't be able to look after a disabled child properly and so looked for someone who could.

All adopted children need to feel good about who they are. Positive knowledge and understanding of their roots helps them to grow and go forward. The nature versus nurture argument is an old one but today few argue that nature doesn't play a strong part in the make-up of a child. Even in the simplest physical terms there are questions for an adoptee such as: Where do I get my curly hair from? Why do I hate baked beans? Why am I good at maths?

• • •

Telling

Telling is something so vital, so important in the growing up of an adopted child that it should not be referred to as 'telling' but as 'knowing'. Of course, I am referring to what is known and talked about within families whose children arrived at under one or two years old. New parents of children older than this need to be prepared to accept, understand and discuss (when asked to) all the circumstances of their children's past, as most of these children will be quite aware they've been moved. With very young children there can be little scope for 'telling'; rather, they need to be made familiar with the words 'adoption' and 'adopted'. We must overcome our own hang-ups, embarrassments and insecurities for our children's sakes. Throwing 'adopted' into your baby talk to an infant in arms may seem clumsy and silly, but it will hardly be heard by anyone but you and your baby, so does it matter? It sows the seeds of knowledge – understanding comes later after all.

There are books that can give the ideal opening to the introduction of a child's individual adoption story. But every child's beginning is different and any of the published children's books will only serve, at this stage, to help parents introduce the subject in an appropriate way for their child.

The best way I've come across of turning 'telling' into 'knowing' for a young child is very cheap and simple: buy one of those small plastic pocket-sized photograph albums that hold one photograph per slot, some plain card (postcards are fine) and some felt-tip pens, and gather up whatever photographs you have managed to acquire through your social worker from your child's first family. You can then make a very simple personalised 'I am adopted' book, adapted and embellished as is right for your child. This will then become part of the library of children's books that all your children can enjoy at any age and stage of their lives.

Adoptive parents should aim for their child to feel that they can't remember being told they were adopted, rather that they have always known, without feeling they was especially odd or different. Whether or not we've succeeded time alone will tell…

Learning about adoption – A cautionary tale

At the age of 18, on a visit to Somerset House to obtain a birth certificate for college, I discovered that I was adopted. It was exceedingly traumatic.

My memories of my childhood were happy. I lived with my father and mother in a terraced council house in London. Other members of the family – grandparents, aunts, cousins – lived in the same street. Throughout my childhood I had feelings that I was different from them all but had no reason to explain why.

My mother became seriously ill when I was 17, the year before I was due to go to college to become a teacher. My father was distraught and one night we had a row in which he said something like: 'You'll never be like my wife, and I don't mean your mother.' This puzzled me, but he would not explain himself and I couldn't understand it. My mother was too ill to ask.

When I was due to go to college I needed a birth certificate. My father said he didn't have one and my mother was still too ill to ask so I decided to get one for myself. I looked but it wasn't there so I asked for assistance. 'Are you adopted?' asked the clerk, barely raising her eyes from the desk. 'No,' I said. 'Well, I suggest you go and look in the Adopted Children's Register,' she said. I did, my heart was pounding and there I found myself. I cannot describe how I felt. I was stunned, faint, sick, my head was swimming – all at once! I couldn't believe it. I wanted to cry but the room was full of people.

I went home and I didn't tell my parents what I had discovered. I didn't tell anyone.

I had a terrible time in my first term at college and my adoptive mother also died during this period. I stole from several students: meaningless objects I did not need. I did nothing with them, just stored them in a drawer. I later went and confessed to my college tutor and it all came out about my adoption. They were very sympathetic and did not send me away, but they insisted that I have psychiatric help, which I did. I went once a week for a year for psychotherapy. It was very helpful. I was able to examine all my feelings about adoption.

In the years since then I have twice sought out more psychotherapy. The feelings were very deep indeed, but I think at the moment that they are all resolved.

Unsupported

We adopted our son as a baby. Our lives were very happy until our son reached his mid-teens.

He started having eating problems and as time went on he became anorexic. He was eventually taken into hospital after trying to cut the fat off his face and stomach. During this time he said that although he had known all along that he was adopted, he would never accept this as the root of his problems. At this time we saw our son going through the trauma of trying to come to terms with who he was, something that was never resolved. He was discharged after ten weeks and told he should be able to manage now; then he was left with no follow-up or support. That time was harrowing for us.

Of course, the eternal question for us is: 'Where did we go wrong?' Should we have ever told him that he was adopted? No one was available for us to talk to and the hospital treated us with indifference. The eating disorder unit at the hospital closed down subsequently. We asked for a social worker to help us but to no avail. Once again our strength was drawn from each other.

After our son was discharged things were fairly stable for a while, but then once again the same pattern emerged. We had one of our family discussions and we all decided to help him find his birth mother. This process has again been very traumatic and painful: on his path of discovery there has been much heartache and at each stage he had to come to terms with hurtful aspects of his birth mother's life. At one stage he was unable to accept that she had had and kept another child only 16 months after giving him away. This was too much and he tried to cut his wrists. Again, we found ourselves dealing with hospitals and psychiatrists. He wanted to continue looking for his birth mother; all he wanted was to see her so that he could know who she was and what she looked like. His two worst fears were that only she and her mother knew of his existence at all and that she might reject him, not wanting anything to do with him. We fully supported our son in his search and from that time we set about in earnest to find out as much as we could. It has taken us just over two years.

We eventually traced our son's birth mother two months ago. A very sensitive approach was taken towards her. We received a phone call from her mother, who said that she didn't want to see him as she had given him up 21 years ago and that was a closed chapter. Also, no one knows of his existence except for the birth mother and her mother. So our son's very worst fears have been realised. He is devastated by this turn of events and now feels he is unable to continue with his life. He has given up work and appears to be unable to help himself.

I do not feel resentment towards his birth mother: at the time she had to give him up because social pressures were different from how they are now. I also feel that she had to go through pain and mental anguish for us to have a baby and has lived with a secret for 21 years. I have spoken to his birth mother to try to reassure her that all he needs is to see her once. I only hope she is able to see her way clear to do that.

The turning point

We have four children in our family: Jenny, aged 20; Sue, aged 18; Francis, aged 16; and Ben, aged 13. This may look like a well-planned family, but it is not quite so. When Sue and Francis were aged seven and five Jenny joined the family; she was then just ten years old. Three years later Ben came to complete our family; he was then six years old. It is part of Ben's life story that I would like to share with you, as I believe that many other families may be able to relate to it and possibly get renewed strength from it.

Ben started to mention his birth mother quite frequently from the age of twelve, which was something he had never done. Previously, if I mentioned anything about his past he would have become either angry or withdrawn, but now we were getting lots of questions. Of course, he did not want to hear the answers I gave, so I was accused of lying about everything: his birth mother really loved him and would have him back if only we would let him go. Things were by then so bad that I felt we had to see if we could arrange a meeting for Ben with his birth mum. I realised that we would be extremely lucky if we could find Ben's social worker six years on, but we were able to do so, and he agreed to arrange a meeting with Ben's birth mum and also to be present at that meeting.

Upon returning home we saw a different side to Ben beginning to emerge; we had the occasional smile and he referred to us occasionally as mum and dad. This improved state of affairs continued for three months, during which time we had our first 'normal' Christmas with Ben – meaning that he was able to spend some of Christmas Day in the same room as the rest of the family. Then we had a huge relapse: all the old behaviour returned, with the addition of physical assaults on me. He was continually asking to go to live in London with his birth mum, so I made a decision which felt dreadful at the time but which has proved to be the turning point in our family's life.

I told Ben that I would write to his mum to see whether he could spend two or three weeks with her during the holidays. During this time we were due to go away for a week's holiday and I just did not want Ben to be with us. I put the question to him: Would he want to take somebody on holiday who did not want to be with him? His answer was: 'No way.' I wrote to his mum, whose reply was: 'Yes.' I then rang her to try to explain why Ben wanted to come and why we felt that it was the best thing for him. I actually said that if he decided that he wanted to stay with her for ever we would not do anything to stop this, but that we hoped he would want to come back to us when he had been given the opportunity to sort out his identity. I firmly believe that it is only when adopted children are able to do this and get an understanding of their past that they are able to start to live in the present and make appropriate attachments in their new family.

We are now once again a family who can have fun and who can laugh; all that went for five years. Most of all, doing what we did has changed Ben: everyone can see the difference and we are always being told what a nice young man he has become. There are still tremendous problems at school, but we feel able to keep on trying for Ben as we now know that he expects us to do all we can to help him. That's another story.

The impact of adoption

This article is about the emotional journey of a young person coming to terms with being adopted.

As a small child, Sam expressed a poignant yearning to have been 'in my tummy' and breastfed like his two elder brothers. The absence of these experiences seemed a significant sadness for him. This appeared to be the only way the knowledge of his adoption impacted on him for the first seven years of his life. There has never been any contact of any kind with his natural parents.

Somewhere between the ages of seven and eight, Sam changed. He became almost uncontrollably angry at times. Most of his anger was directed at me – he withdrew from personal contact and would move as far as possible from me when upset. He began yearning for his mother, and at times said he would run away and find her. When he was very distressed he said he wanted to die. At the time, we were all very muddled and didn't understand what was happening to us. Looking back, and having read about other adopted children with similar experiences, I believe that, at about seven or eight, he became able to conceptualise the loss of his natural mother and was filled with a mixture of pain and rage at his abandonment, these emotions being directed at me. Simultaneously, he became very worried about any separation from me. A school residential trip was only just bearable for him. If I was unexpectedly late home he became very anxious and thought I had died. His performance at school deteriorated significantly. He became difficult for us to discipline, acting as if he believed that we were not his real parents and so had no right to tell him how to behave. He identified with his 'other' family. He fantasised about his 'real brothers and sisters' and distanced himself from our family by assuming mannerisms he felt identified him with them.

It took us at least a year to come to terms with his relating so strongly to another mother and possibly a whole family out there. We, too, were mourning the loss of our exclusive relationship with him and coming to terms with him having left us in some way. We turned to our local social services adoption unit for help – but received none. We then found Adoption UK – who were brilliant – and, through them, The National Organisation for Counselling Adoptees and their Parents (NORCAP). Sam was, by then, nine years old and NORCAP advised against trying to find his mother till he was older. We contacted his adoption agency; they were very off-putting but said that there was no message there for him. Because of his need to find his mother, we decided reluctantly to go ahead the next summer holidays, though as we thought through the practicalities we saw the potential for great distress for him and his mother. As we started talking through the process with him he seemed to back off from pursuing this line.

During the years from nine to twelve, Sam's behaviour at middle school was problematic. At home he seemed like a smouldering volcano, always ready to erupt into aggressive language or behaviour. At around 12, I believe he started to re-identify with and reintegrate into our family. He chose to change schools to one he had previously refused but where his two older brothers went. He became increasingly able to concentrate at school. There have been no complaints about his behaviour. It is as if some inner tension has been resolved.

Sam is now 14. He is loving, affectionate and really happy – and so are we (at our best times!). In between, the normal tensions of family life with a teenager have to be negotiated. Sam has just started wanting to find his natural family again, but this is something we will be doing together, not apart.

We finally meet the birth parents

Five and a half years ago, at the first meeting about the adoption of our children, Nigel and I asked if we could meet our children's birth parents. You'd think we'd asked to meet the Devil himself. 'Oh, you don't want to see them, not a good idea!' Three and a half years after that first meeting, following two court cases, ongoing but irregular contact with siblings, meetings with one birth father and the maternal grandparents, and 'letter box' contact with all and sundry, we finally got to adopt our three wonderful children. We still hadn't met their birth mother and the father of our youngest two, and it looked as though we never would.

However, life and circumstances change constantly – social workers making contact orders, please note – and our children's birth parents had another child and were allowed to care for him. But fate took a tragic twist and their little boy died at 16 months of leukaemia when mum was eight months pregnant with their next child. Their son's death shook us and we felt deeply for them. We decided to write and send a sympathy card besides our normal 'letter box' letters. Their first letter to us followed the birth of their daughter and we wrote back asking if we could meet them.

It took a while, but finally in May we got to meet them. It was arranged and took place at NCH Action For Children at Sutton Coalfield, who were marvellous and also provided some excellent sandwiches! We had decided to arrive early, but so had the birth parents and our first meeting took place in the car park. Our social worker had told us to have a good chat about what we wanted from the meeting and what to expect, and this was good advice. One of the thoughts that had crossed our minds was that their baby was now ten months old – the age our youngest child had been when we got her – and that they might be similar. Therefore, it came as no surprise when the birth mum handed me a beautiful replica of my own child to cuddle. Our social worker wisely told us not to lose sight of the past nor of why our children were adopted, and with this in the back of our minds the meeting went very well.

Lots of information was exchanged; we saw lots of photos and were promised copies. All our questions and more were answered and hopefully we answered lots of theirs. The meeting lasted over two hours, and towards the end the birth mum stated how much the children looked like us and that perhaps it was all meant to be. This got me all emotional, hugs were exchanged and when they left they told the social workers how happy they were that it was us who had adopted their children.

Of course, there were aspects of the meeting which reminded us of why our children were adopted, but we gained so much from it, and although we did not need to seek their birth mother's blessing, we came out of the meeting feeling that the children were even more our children. We are so pleased that we finally got to meet them; we feel sure it will help us and our children in the future. And now when my daughter asks, 'What time was I born at, Mum?', I can answer her correctly.

Calling her bluff

Our daughter is 11 years of age and she has been with us since she was seven months old. We have always answered questions about her adoption and birth mother as she has asked them.

When she was younger, we told her that the reason why her mum did not look after her was that she had some problems and could not manage to look after a child. As she got older and asked what these problems were, we explained that there was an alcohol problem, that when she had come to us at seven months old she only weighed about eight pounds and that she had been left in the house on her own and was totally neglected.

Over the past nine or ten months our daughter has been talking about how, now that she is bigger and can look after herself, she could go back to her birth mother. I have explained very gently and patiently, giving her lots of reassurance about our love for her as our 'special daughter', how she could not go back at this time to her birth mother. Eventually, it came to the crunch.

One evening at the dinner table she again brought up the subject, and again we were going through the explanations of why she couldn't go and how more than anything she was our little girl and we cared very much about what happened to her – but nothing would stop her in her persistent tirade.

Eventually, I told her very calmly that if that was what she wanted to do then she could think about it while she cleared the table, and dad and I would go into the living room and she could come and let us know what she felt.

For the next few minutes all I could think was: 'What have I done? What if she says she wants to go?' But deep down I felt very calm. Maybe there was a bit of me that felt that our daughter was enjoying holding this over us, although we had never made an issue of it.

Our daughter came to the living room door as though nothing had happened, and I asked what she wanted to do now. She said that she was going nowhere but here. I cuddled her and told her how glad I was as I would have been very unhappy for her and for us if she had wanted to go. We never once said that she had to go or that we wanted her to go or that we didn't want her any more. There had been no rejection from us.

This all happened about two months ago and our daughter has been reassured that she can still talk about her birth mum and ask any questions she wants. All I was hoping to stop were the threats and manipulation, which were no good for us as a family and were anything but positive for her. Now we can only look forward to the future and the next issue with hope.

Biting the bullet

Ellie was two and a half years old when we adopted her. For a while things continued very positively and every few weeks we would reflect and say, 'Look what she has achieved.' At home she was always the little girl with the curl (when she was good…), even though sometimes I noticed that we did not seem special to her and she appeared to love everyone. She found close relationships difficult and hated any change of routine. In front of others her self-control was perfect while with us she could change from Jekyll to Hyde in a split second. As she got older her tantrums gained momentum and she could be violent. She had 'letter box' contact with her mother but the letters contained little information other than, 'I love you, I miss you.'

By the time she was nine her tantrums had become public as well as private. Ellie didn't care who saw her when she was in a rage and I was at my wits' end.

I felt it was time to bite the bullet. I knew that what I was going to say could backfire but I felt so defeated that I was willing to take that chance. Looking into the years ahead I knew that I couldn't carry on like this. I had turned from being a bouncy, positive, 'the bumps are what you climb on' type of person into an emotionally exhausted wreck, never knowing when she was next going to blow.

I explained that while onlookers might overlook a toddler having a tantrum, people seeing that type of behaviour from an older girl might report me to the police or social services, thinking that I was possibly an abductor or at least mistreating her.

I explained that she was a very intelligent girl with a lot of choices – bright at school and with a supportive family, she had the potential to be whatever she wanted to be. If her behaviour continued in this vein we were at risk of outside intervention, over which we may have no control. We may lose our choices – she may lose her choices.

Next (and how I battled internally over this), I began to discuss her early life, and told her that while her birth mother loved her, her birth mother also had choices and had not always made the choices which were right for both of them.

I explained that we could get out her files and read what had happened – and that it might not be a nice story. She listened to and digested that information. The next day we read her file together. (I did miss out a couple of the worst bits.)

It was magical, as if a spell had been broken. How long would it last? Our 'little girl with the curl' disappeared. The 'very, very good' became pleasant, down-to-earth good, and when she was bad she was no longer over the top. And so it has continued. Her guilt seems gone, for now at least. She has stopped cuddling strangers.

Most importantly, she no longer pushes us away, and our relationship has progressed and deepened very much as a result.

It is now a year since that night – a night when I reached the depths of despair and yet which proved a catalyst in our relationship. As time goes by I am regaining my optimism and feel that any further setbacks – which must surely come with the teenage years – may possibly prove easier to deal with.

Last week Ellie told me, 'I'm really happy. I *like* myself now.' I have never seen Ellie looking so relaxed over such a sustained period – she now looks like a 'complete' child and says that, for the first time, she feels like one too!

CHAPTER 14

Tracing

For many adoptees there comes a time when talking and wondering about their birth families is not enough. They want to trace their birth parents, to find their physical roots. As one adoptee said: 'You have to know and understand your family roots. It is difficult to have a future without having had a past.'

For some adoptees, tracing their birth parents today is a matter of a few phone calls to social workers; for others, adopted during those years when all links with a birth family were severed on the day of adoption, the search can take years and sometimes prove fruitless.

Tracing can be fraught with problems. Although many birth mothers greet the child they gave up for adoption 20, 30 or even 40 years earlier with open arms, others have carried the birth of their adopted child as a secret for so long that they cannot cope with the ramifications of a grown-up daughter or son appearing on their doorstep. Every adoptee who traces has a different story to tell.

For those who do succeed, a meeting can provide the pieces that always seemed missing in the puzzle of their lives. Many adoptees are astonished by the instant recognisability of their birth parents when they meet. One adoptee said: 'My birth mother looked just like me only 20 years older. It was like looking into a time mirror.'

But even at its best, the meeting between birth parent and child is an emotionally fraught experience for all concerned in the adoption triangle: the adoptee meeting the parents who gave them life but then for whatever reason could not keep them; the adoptive parent who feels emotionally threatened by their child's desire to find their 'other' parents; and the birth parent coming face to face with a child that they were unable to bring up themselves.

To help and counsel adult adoptees who wish to trace their birth parents, NORCAP was set up in 1982. NORCAP provides support for adoptees and both their birth and adoptive parents in the process of tracing and meeting one another. Pamela Hodgkins, one of the group's founders and an adoptee herself, says that her research shows that for most adoptees tracing has been a rewarding experience. Often, finding half-brothers and sisters as well as a birth mother is a major part of that reward. Research by her on behalf of NORCAP also shows that those who have traced have good relationships with their adoptive parents – they are their family. As one adoptee said after tracing her birth mother, 'I have got two very caring mothers – but only one mum.'

• • •

Now he has two mums

Our son joined our family as a permanent placement when he was 12. He came into care aged four and had not seen any of his natural family since then. We were his seventh placement. We spent four very traumatic years with our son. He managed to overcome chronic enuresis, kleptomania and romantically told 'tall stories'.

When he was 16 he asked me one evening out of the blue: 'Mum, why can't I see my mum?' I realised instantly that we had hardly discussed his mother in four years, but that he was very settled and a real member of our family, and I quickly answered: 'I don't see why you shouldn't see her – if she agrees to it.' I phoned his social worker the next morning. She knew the whereabouts of his mother and promised to investigate. His mother agreed to meet him and the social worker on neutral ground.

Our son was very calm and understood that he should not entertain any illusions; it might just be a one-off meeting. Mother and son did not instantly like each other. In fact, his mother was reminded of bad times years ago and felt quite sure that she could never take to our son as a person. This I explained to him as delicately as I could. But we did invite his mother to visit us when she felt like it. This visit took place some months later. An older sister who had always lived with her came too, and everyone remarked on how much like a natural family they looked. They realised that they were all sensible adults who could act like a family even if it was going to take a long time to bond.

Now, four years later, our son is 20 years old and is in the armed forces. When on leave he divides his time between the two mums' places. I do his washing, our other boys help him to maintain his motorbike and his 'real' mother is a better cook than I am! Although the two mothers have completely different lifestyles, we do confide over the phone and understand each other, and our son, who seems very relaxed, has of course the best of both worlds. One could find faults: is there a lack of commitment on all sides? I don't think it matters.

Mother and child reunion

Thirty-eight years after my adoption, being happily married with two children and with my adoptive parents still living in the house where I grew up with a caring and loving family, I decided that my birth mother had the right to know that I was alright and that I had always admired, respected and even loved her for having to make possibly the most traumatic decision in her life.

I was counselled by my social worker, who gave me examples of the worst and best possible outcomes of the search. The counselling session was quite emotional for me and I suppose the reality of what I was about to do was beginning to sink in. My parents were quite happy for me to search but worried about what effect all this would have on my birth mother's life, particularly if she had not mentioned it to her husband. I too was concerned for her and knew the letter would have to be very carefully worded.

First, I sent for my birth certificate. On Friday 29 January it arrived. I decided to find out whether my birth mother's parents still lived at that address. They didn't – a Mr and Mrs S lived there. I asked a friend to ring saying that she needed to get in touch with my birth mother (using her name) to invite her to an ex-colleague's retirement party and asking if they by any chance knew her or her family. The response was: 'I know her mum well, her sister lives over the road – I'll get the address for you.' I went into total shock. I couldn't believe that by midday the search was over. By Saturday I had the address and phone number. Thirty-six hours, two notepads and a tense headache later the letter was ready to be sent.

I had enclosed a postcard for her to return so I would at least know that she had received the information I had sent. Before I received this she rang to cancel what she had written on the card, which had been that she wanted to meet me as soon as possible. Thankfully (for me), she had told her husband about me, but my letter had caused a rift in the family. I was devastated but she tried to reassure me that it wasn't me, it was just the final straw, and so she felt she would not be able to cope with meeting me so soon. But the next day she rang to say the rift had been solved and she and her mother would be in town by 1.30 p.m. I was in a panic. I would be meeting my mother in two and a half hours; my stomach churned at the thought of it. I couldn't think of what I was going to say to this person I had never met before and yet felt I knew. I stood by the meeting place and watched everybody wearing a cream blouse and brooch. (I have never seen so many people wearing that colour blouse in my life.) Then, coming towards me in the distance I saw a lady I knew was my mother. I ran to her and gave her a big hug, with the words: 'I've found you.' During the conversation that followed it became apparent that my birth mother's husband was obviously feeling threatened by my turning up and I decided that I must reassure him, when I met him, that I did not want to be a threat to him or the family – all I wanted was to be able to write to my birth mother as and when I felt like it. After all, I have my family and all the childhood memories that go with being part of that family, and I may have two very caring mothers, but I only have one mum.

The two hours passed quickly. They gave me a lift home and that was the search completely finished – from the start to the meeting had taken 22 days. I was completely numb. One thing that has remained in my mind is that my birth mother asked me why it had taken me so long. I tried to explain that had I done it earlier I would not have been mature enough to handle all the emotions that one takes on when one ventures into such a task, and that as a teenager it would have been for the wrong reasons. It's only since becoming a mother that I've realised how torn I would have been had I had to give up my children for adoption and feel that I would have always wondered how they were. She accepted my explanation, but I feel that the only person who has truly suffered over the years has been her, with maybe a knock-on effect on her family. The following week she and her husband came to see me and my family along with one of her sisters and her mother. It was all lovely. But I thought the situation was being taken out of my birth mother's hands, so in the next letter I wrote to her I passed on what I considered to be sound information given to me by my social worker, and that was never to let anyone make you go faster than you are prepared to go or enter into a situation you are not comfortable with. She was pleased I had taken the pressure off her.

Three months have passed. My birth mother and her husband have now met my parents and have seen where I grew up. Both my mothers share the same interests and have visited the same places abroad; it is incredible how social workers matched my parents so well.

I realise now that my birth mother's need for me to find her was greater than mine. I'm pleased that I decided to do the search. All the emotions I have gone through have been worthwhile. At least now she can have peace of mind and the relationship we have can be built on taking one step at a time.

Update 1999: Sadly, my parents were both killed in a car accident, and when my birth mother was told her reply was: 'Well, that's all right, she has me.' For weeks after she would phone me, but couldn't understand why I was still grieving when she was my mother.

In quiet moments when I'm thinking about my parents I also reflect back on the situation of my birth mother. First, I feel that perhaps my search for my birth mother was also to fulfil a need of my mum's. She was the one who would often say, 'How I wish I could let your mother know...' Second, the other thing that comes to mind is a comment my birth mother made when she was thinking clearly: 'You were allowed to blossom outwards; all I could do was go in on myself.'

I still have great respect and love for my birth mother, but unfortunately I will not and cannot allow her to be *my mother* nor let her rule me as she has been ruled by her own mother. She was never allowed to talk about me or even to grieve. My birth mother has been a victim of her era.

Tracing: My parents couldn't understand

I was adopted as a baby of six weeks and grew up in South London in a normal, happy, middle-class family. But despite the happiness and the uneventful childhood, there were always those nagging questions at the back of my mind. Who was I before I was adopted and why didn't my birth parents keep me? It was not until I married and had children of my own that I felt compelled to discover some of the answers. When, at antenatal clinic, you are asked things such as, 'Is there a history of diabetes or heart trouble in your family?', you simply cannot give an answer if you do not know anything about the people who brought you into this world.

After the birth of my second son my husband and I set out to find out more about my background. We found my birth mother. That was many years ago and since then we have kept in regular contact. My birth mother's three brothers and their families know all about me. I have met them all many times and I am accepted by them as one of the family, despite having been an embarrassing dark secret for so long.

And what of mum and dad – the people who brought me up and devoted their lives to me? At first mum could not understand why I needed to know about my past, let alone trace my birth mother. She felt threatened and assumed that I might find my birth family more attractive or more exciting, or simply want to be with them more than I did with her. Nothing could be further from the truth. In recent years she has felt more able to talk about it and to try to understand my feelings. In short, she now feels more secure about the relationships involved. Dad, unfortunately, could never accept the circumstances of adoption. As far as he was concerned I was his daughter and that was it. There was nothing more to say on the matter.

Although I am grateful for having traced my birth mother and for the continuing contact with her, I feel no reason to love her. Yes, she is a thoroughly likeable, decent lady and it is astounding to see how much we are alike. Most importantly, I now know my roots. For me it was important to know who I was and where I came from. Having discovered that, I could get on with the rest of my life.

The anguish of the adoptive parents

We were given the name of adoptive parents 26 years ago but the word adoptive seemed to have disappeared from our minds until very recently, when our son finally went ahead and traced his birth mother. The resulting trauma took both my husband and I by complete surprise. After all, we were aware that the law had changed in 1975 to allow adopted people to do this, and on many occasions over the years had said to each other and to other people that this would be a perfectly natural thing to do and if the roles were reversed we would certainly want to know about our origins and roots.

Our son first showed an interest in tracing his birth mother when he was 17 and the process took nine years to complete. Emotional crises in his life seemed to be the trigger which on three occasions motivated him into taking his enquiries one stage further, until this year he actually traced and met his birth mother for the first time. Fortunately for us he is a kind and caring lad who discussed everything with us from the start. We in turn helped and encouraged him, warned him of all the possible pitfalls and, in our innocence, assured him genuinely that we would not be hurt in any way.

Why then did we experience a kind of total system-shock? Before our son had traced and met his birth mother we were able to accept the situation, but when it happened we were extremely upset. As his mother for 26 years, seeing a letter my son was given in which his birth mother had written 'If my son attempts to contact me I would be more than happy' caused very painful emotions – emotions which I had to hide as he was obviously on 'cloud nine'. Of course, I was happy for him and pleased that when they met it was better than he had expected and that, in his words, he felt that the jigsaw was completed. He was so euphoric that in no way could I mar things by letting him see the depth of the devastation I felt inside.

Our eldest daughter (also adopted) was very aware of my anguish, and probably because she is a mother of two children herself she was more able to identify with my feelings than our youngest (our natural daughter), who doesn't live locally. Even so, both were very supportive. I was bombarded by every emotion under the sun, totally out of control as everything was purely emotional, and logical thought disappeared out of the window. Also, the façade I presented to my son was difficult to maintain. At this point, my husband said casually to our son, 'Just ask your counsellor, in her experience, if it's normal to feel a little upset in our position.' After the next meeting with her he told us that she'd said, 'Yes, of course; in fact, your parents have taken it very well – some people are devastated.' She also said that she would be happy to talk to us. Our subsequent talk helped tremendously and her words struck many chords, so that I began to feel a little less abnormal and ashamed of my adverse reaction.

I hope our experiences will help others starting out on this journey. Adoptive parents must request help when tracing begins in order to be prepared to cope with the emotions it arouses.

Searching for roots

Our first adoption took place in 1980. John is severely disabled: his left arm is missing above elbow level and he has short, very deformed legs. (His right leg was subsequently amputated when he was nine.) We were asked to care for him when he was eight months old 'to see if he can fit into a family'. He had spent the whole of his life until then in hospital, as he had been born extremely prematurely – according to estimates, his gestation lasted about 25 to 26 weeks. We were told by the specialist, 'He'll never walk, he'll never crawl, he'll never sit, he'll never stand, he's profoundly deaf and severely mentally handicapped. Just take him home and love him.' We had not yet seen this child, so you can imagine how we felt. We approached his hospital cot with trepidation, to be greeted by the biggest smile and the cheekiest pair of brown eyes you could possibly imagine! It later transpired that John had been assessed according to his chronological age, with no account being taken of his prematurity.

We took him home and loved him. By ten months he was sitting unaided. By 12 months he was dragging himself along the floor. At 15 months he climbed from pouffe to table and on to the top of the piano. By 18 months he was walking, talking and getting into as much mischief as the average 18-month-old child!

Because John's mother had been very young – she had had her sixteenth birthday only three weeks before his birth – she felt unable to cope with a baby and requested that he be placed for adoption. This was a decision from which she never wavered, although her boyfriend offered to support them both.

The search to find him a new family had been ongoing, but with the medical prognosis so damning it was proving to be almost impossible. One family showed an interest, but when they were offered a newborn 'perfect' baby John was back 'on the market'. This we couldn't bear. We quizzed his social worker. 'Is there any chance of our being allowed to adopt John?' Her beaming reply was: 'I thought you'd never ask!' It seems that 'they' had already decided that John would be best staying with us but were waiting for us to make the first move! So, three years after he first came to live with us, the adoption order was made.

One day I am going to write a book about all the delights of our life as parents. It may run to three or four volumes! It is sufficient to say that we adopted John: we made no secret of the fact and over the years he has been told everything we know about his birth family. He has never felt a burning desire to meet them but circumstances have recently set him questioning about his birth father. His questions are along the lines of, 'Who do I look like?', and, 'Is my condition hereditary?' (You might guess from this that girls, and one in particular, are involved!)

An initial visit to social services elicited the response, 'You know more than I have got on this introductory file!' We now await the production of the full file, although because John is at university that won't be until his next visit home, probably at Christmas. In the meantime, because we still live in the same area as John's family, he is quietly accumulating more information.

At no time have we felt threatened by John's interest in his origins. This may be because we have a very close and loving relationship with him and he tells us very openly how he feels about everything (except his current girlfriend – it must be serious!).

In this case it has been beneficial that we reside in the same area as the birth family. To those of you who have feelings of trepidation about your child searching for their roots, think about all the skeletons in your family's cupboard and the feelings some of the older members of your family might have if you started digging. Within us there is often a desperate need to know more about our roots. How much stronger this must be in our children, who do not have blood relatives with whom to share family 'secrets'.

CHAPTER 15

The Birth Mother's Story

Until recently, birth parents were the forgotten side of the adoption triangle. If remembered they were often regarded with disapproval: they had 'given away' their children or had parenting skills that were considered so inadequate and/or abusive that the child had been removed from them. Their vulnerability, their sensitivity and the emotional attachment they felt for the child from whom they had parted were disregarded. For whatever reason it seemed that birth mothers could be – and some felt should be – ignored.

But today's adopters realise that the birth parents cannot and must not be forgotten, whatever the circumstances of a child's arrival in a foster or adoptive home.

'Our birth parents are responsible for the way each of us look, our tastes and our talents, which are all in our genes,' said one adoptive mother. 'Nothing can change that. We all need to feel good about our physical roots. If an adoptive parent cannot empathise or sympathise with the circumstances that brought a child into care, they should not adopt that child.'

'Adoptive parents generally see us as a possible threat,' said Doreen Ward, a founder member of the birth mothers' Natural Parents Network, 'and the birth mother is full of fears that she is inadequate and not as good as the adopters. There is a lot of fantasy, envy and jealousy on both sides. But really that shouldn't be. You both love the child and you are always connected because of the child.'

She believes that fantasy and fear are made worse when birth parent and adoptive parent know nothing of each other. 'Fears vanish and the sense of being different diminishes once you meet.'

The Natural Parents Network was set up in 1987 and today has more than 500 members between the ages of 20 and 80, most of whom, through circumstances that were at the time beyond their control, gave up a child for adoption.

'The traditional view was that we should go away, get on with our lives and forget, but most of us don't. It takes years to get over the loss of a child through adoption. Parents who have just been separated from their children are very angry and distraught. Some are desperate to show the world that they are mothers and get pregnant again very quickly; others are made to feel so inadequate by the experience that they find it difficult ever to get pregnant again,' said Doreen.

The years don't eliminate the loss. 'There are certain days when memories are more sharply in focus – such as birthdays. Those are the days when birth mothers need other birth mothers to talk to.'

But the imaginary picture of a birth child given up for adoption growing up is increasingly being replaced by the real person. 'Ten years ago just one or two of the mothers belonging to our group had contact with their birth children. They were rarities. Today between half and two-thirds of them have had some contact with their birth child,' said Doreen. 'The climate of opinion has changed dramatically and post-adoption centres have also made an enormous difference. Birth mothers are exploring the possibilities of contact and far more adopted people are searching.'

The difficulty for birth mothers – as for adopters in other aspects of adoption – is that the response they get from different social services agencies and different social workers varies dramatically. 'It is an ad hoc situation. There are no set guidelines. One birth mother who is a member of the group knew that her son had made contact with the agency, wanting to find out more about her when he was 17. When he was 19 she approached the agency and was told that no contact could be made until he approached the agency again. She had sufficient determination to call back a couple of days later and pursue the matter – a different social worker answered the phone who had an entirely different point of view and within a matter of days contact had been opened up,' said Doreen.

'There is a completely groundless fear that the birth mother is going to knock on the door of their now-adopted child and say, "Hi! I'm your long lost mum," But nothing could be further from the truth. Most birth mothers are terrified of that first contact, and many have taken years to overcome feelings of inadequacy or anger due to their having had to give up a child or having had a child taken away from them.'

Today, when a child comes into care, adoptive parents are usually given a very full picture of the catalogue of circumstances that brought them to adoption. It is increasingly rare that some link with a child's birth family, however tenuous, is not suggested.

But Doreen would like to see more changes. 'When adoption becomes an option the birth mother is taken over: having her child adopted is usually a decision made for her rather than with her. That is not healthy and is why many birth mothers end up feeling angry and victimised. It is not good to feel a victim. It is better if they feel a part of what is happening and partly responsible for it. Their opinions and thoughts are valuable.'

The problems, personalities and talents of the birth parents often get lost or are ignored in the process of a child being placed for adoption. 'But those talents and characteristics – whether they are creative, athletic, quick-witted, oversensitive, strong-minded, tough, sickly…whatever – are also part of the genetic make-up of the child. Somebody – not necessarily the person at the sharp edge of the adoption – needs to take the time to understand the person behind the problem. It could give all sorts of keys to the child going into care and help to create a successful placement for the child and a greater understanding of that child.'

This is the birth mother's story.

• • •

Letter from a birth mother

Dear Mr and Mrs Wakefield,

I just wanted to say thank you for supporting Natalie in her decision to find me, and to reassure you about my own reasons for wanting to meet her.

I can remember reading an open letter in a women's magazine from a woman who'd given up her baby for adoption years earlier and hadn't ever seen him again. She said that she was 'grateful' to the couple who had adopted him for 'bringing him up for me'.

I don't agree with that: you brought Natalie up for her and for yourselves, and made a far better job of it than I would have given my situation. She is your daughter, it was you who sat up in the night with her, comforted her when she fell over, treasured her first crayon pictures from school, and all the other million and one things that make a family. You are her mum and dad.

I am looking forward very much to meeting her, not because I want to see my 'missing' baby, not because I want to call myself her mother, but because I gave her to you from love. I have never forgotten her, and I want to meet the young woman that she has grown into and, if she wants it, to become friends with her.

I have never forgotten, either, how very kind and understanding you were to me all those years ago, and please believe me when I say I would do nothing to hurt you now. All I want is Natalie's happiness, and if that means including me in her life as a friend, that will make me happy also.

I suppose what I am saying is that I am not hoping to have my missing baby back, I am hoping to make a new friend of this person who is so very precious to you, and that I will bring a new and happy dimension to her life, but not replace what she already has.

I do hope this makes sense. I'd be lying if I said I didn't love her, even though I haven't met her yet. I've loved her since before she was born, and time and distance do nothing to change that. But loving means letting go, and I did that 24 years ago, and I don't intend to try to 'take back' now.

Thank you for your care and compassion all those years ago, and thank you for your understanding now. You are very special people.

Amnesia was the prescription: A birth mother speaks

Twenty-five years ago, at the age of 19, I became pregnant and was unmarried. I was sacked from my job as a student nurse and left my parents' house to live some 60 miles away.

I gave birth to a healthy daughter whom I breastfed for the first four weeks of her life – one of the rules of the house: we all breastfed. She was then weaned onto the bottle in preparation for adoption at six weeks. The decision to have her adopted had been made at the beginning of the pregnancy and confirmed at an interview with an adoption agency social worker when she was four weeks old. The interview lasted ten minutes. At no time did anybody ask me how I felt about parting with a child for adoption, and I left the mother and baby home to start a 'new life' having been made to feel that I was now expected to act as if nothing had happened.

And that is what I believed I was doing for the next 22 years – refusing to understand the message of the post-natal depression after the birth of my son, the feelings of tension whenever I saw my parents, what was making me cry at certain pieces of music, and the guilt that was continually displaced onto other things in my life.

Two years ago I saw an advertisement in a newspaper for a meeting in London for women who had parted with children for adoption. I rang the number (of the Post-Adoption Centre) to ask if there was something similar in the North of England and was told that there wasn't (though there is now), but why didn't I come down to London and see if I could get something from this meeting? I arrived rather early and so had a chance to look around the centre at the posters and publications. As I looked and tried to read, an amazing feeling came over me: I was there because I really had given birth to a baby all those years ago. That realisation grew and grew during the evening as I cried and held hands with other women who were as frightened and excited as I by the route they were starting to travel that night.

The group continues to meet. Many feelings have emerged during these last two years: deep grief, anger, outrage, joy, and the realisation that perhaps somewhere there is an adult who has a life of her own, not a six-week-old baby frozen in time. It amazes me that I could have kept all this buried for so long. But how else would I and all the women like me have managed to survive in a society that has refused to recognise our existence? We have been invisible to our adopted children, professionals, authors and each other.

Some of us have now become sufficiently confident in ourselves and the views that we hold on the needs of birth mothers, both past and future, that we are beginning to speak out at conferences on adoption practice. We believe that we have experienced a particular sort of bereavement that cannot be resolved because there has been neither a death nor any of the rituals that accompany death. Instead, we have to keep adjusting to the loss of a growing person, and that often means putting painful fantasies into the void where that person should be. If some sort of contact is maintained, even if it is only the occasional piece of news about the lost son or daughter, how much more real the relationship will seem. For the birth mothers whom I know, one piece of news or one photograph would have felt very open compared to the total lack of acknowledgement of our motherhood that we have experienced. No wonder some reunions are so traumatic when two people who are the closest of relatives and yet complete strangers are trying to build together something that they believe should be present.

When my child disappeared at the age of six weeks it felt final and my feelings of self-worth were extremely low, almost as if I had caused the death of my own child. Because I had given her away I deserved nothing, and being given no information about her has reinforced my own view of myself as being undeserving and powerless. I was encouraged to be a mother who cared so much for her child that she would give her to a family who were going to be the perfect parents that she couldn't be.

Update 1999: Three years after writing this article my daughter and I met, and we have maintained contact over the years since then. We have been through some very difficult times and some equally rewarding and happy times. I believe that we have both gained from having the opportunity to know each other.

Nobody listened

I was 17 years old when I had my baby daughter. I had been in care myself for a number of years and when I got pregnant a lot of people tried to convince me that I should have an abortion – but I wanted to have my baby, so then they tried to convince me that I should have her adopted.

My daughter was born on a Tuesday. I had her at ten o'clock in the morning and by 11 o'clock they had sent in an adoption agent to try to convince me to give her up. Five days later they took her into care because they couldn't find a place that would have us both. But I didn't give her up. It took me seven weeks and then I got a bedsit of my own, collected my baby daughter and hardly put her down for weeks because I was so overjoyed.

But she wasn't an easy baby. Almost from the day she was born my daughter was different from other children and difficult to handle. If anyone else ever looked after her once, that was enough – they wouldn't have her back. When she was two she went to nursery and kept getting sent out for her bad behaviour. I asked for help with an increasingly difficult, angry toddler. But no one listened to me. They told me nothing was wrong with my child; I was just a young and inexperienced mother and I should go away.

Every year I had more and more difficulties with her head-bashing, stripping, screaming and tantrums. No one would babysit for her. Constant arguing and stealing started. At four and a half she went to school. The first day it was heaven and I could shop without a child throwing a tantrum. Then she started lying and stealing from school. After her first term I received a letter requesting me to go in to see the headmistress. She said my daughter was unbearable to have in the school and suggested that she see a psychologist and go to special school. I was worried. I thought a psychologist would help.

Three months later we started to see a doctor. I told her the whole story and situation. I wanted some help. I had tried everything I knew of. I knew there was something wrong with my daughter. One doctor told us that my daughter's behaviour was something within her but that she would grow out of it and that there was nothing I could have done about it.

Her anger was frightening. Her tantrums would make her pass out. She was this screaming, angry ball of temper tantrum. But everyone blamed me for her behaviour. A new psychiatrist decided to try to get all of us admitted and then decided that I was too angry a person and that while I was angry they would be unable to help my daughter. This was the last thing in the world I wanted. After a year social services said that unless I signed my daughter into voluntary care they would get a court order.

Very involuntarily, I voluntarily signed her into care. I had to choose the lesser of the two evils. If I signed her into voluntary care I still had parental rights. I tried to play as smart a game with them as possible. At the time I was pregnant again – my son was born while my daughter was in care.

When my son was three months old I was called to a meeting at my daughter's foster parents' home. There, a senior social worker told me they were applying for a full care order. I cried and screamed and shouted. I left the foster parents and went to her school. When I got there they had already taken her. I was gutted.

But I got to see her and as time went on she would sneak out of school to see me. We got on during visits and she wanted to come home and I wanted her home. It was heartbreaking.

In the end the case came up and that was hard for me. I had no family. I was on my own with my son. In the court the judge gave me six months to start therapy. I did everything social services said. We went back to court six months later. But I fell apart. That was it. They kept her. She was nearly seven years old.

One day when she came to visit me she brought a book about the woman who was going to adopt her. I photocopied the book and gave it back. I felt that I hated this woman. I looked at her and thought, 'You can't have my daughter.' She was eight when she went to live with this woman. But I knew where she was and had the phone number. I remember calling her and telling her to look in the garden for a can of Coke I had hidden for her so that she knew I knew where she was.

I didn't make any contact with her adoptive mother. There were times when I didn't contact her. I was so depressed. Two weeks before every birthday I would cry constantly.

When my daughter was 13 she ran away from her adoptive mother. The police knocked on my door. Eventually, she was found in Leicester, and either my daughter or her adoptive mother asked for respite. Social services placed her two or three miles away from me. After one week I got a letter from my daughter and went to the house where she was staying immediately. I drove up and down but didn't knock on the door. She had sent me a telephone number and I called her. Ten minutes later we met up the road.

At first we saw each other sneakily but then social services said we could get in touch officially. I broke down in tears.

My daughter is in a children's home at the moment. She has lots of problems and won't accept help. She is a very angry young lady. She has a big jealousy problem with her brother. In her eyes she was kicked out for him when he was born.

After she ran away I met her adoptive mother at her house. Even though I knew she didn't take my child away, I felt strange in her domain. We argued about whose daughter she was. My daughter had lived with me for five years and with her for five years. She had tried her hardest.

It has now been confirmed that my daughter has a hereditary problem called Asperger's syndrome. I was relieved and angry when I found out. I had always said there was something wrong with her. At the moment she doesn't want to see me. Nothing will shift her until she wants to be shifted. I hope our relationship works out. I know she is still angry. The best thing I can do is sit back and wait.

I have a lovely relationship with my son and I wish I had that with my daughter. Underneath it all she is not a bad kid. She is brainy. She could do well. She is good at sport and arts and music. She sat her GCSEs recently. She just runs away from her problems.

My son and his mum and dad

I get upset that someone else is calling my son their son. I have often wondered what the word 'adoption' really means to the parties of the adoption triangle. To the birth mother it means losing all her parental rights, but it cannot mean that her child does not exist any more. To the child it seems to mean that he or she has a new family and a new name, but still has a genetic history that adoption cannot change. To the adoptive parents it seems to mean that they are the parents of children who come to them with an extra package – their past.

After 32 years of ill health, I approached my son's adoptive family because I did not know what had happened to him; among other things, I often wondered if he was still alive. If he had died, no one would have taken the trouble to find me and tell me.

When I had my family of two more children, they did not replace my lost child. He will always be the special individual that he is.

I know that in my son's heart his adoptive mother is his true mother and the feelings he has for me are different. We love each other, but more like a brother and sister or aunt and nephew. I am great friends with his parents and they welcome me with open arms every time I visit their home. Our son still lives with his adoptive parents because they are all happy together and they are his true family. I would not destroy what they have created for each other; that is sacred. I am grateful for that, and I feel privileged to see at first hand the bond they have with each other. If I could have only known that years ago my life would have been a lot better.

Despite this wonderful reunion I still cry for my lost baby. I have lost 32 years of his life, but I try to make sense of all of this by saying to myself that I gave those years to his parents. Because they have welcomed me with open arms I cannot begrudge what they have together.

It is six years since I made my approach to them, and at the time I did feel a lot of guilt. Looking back, I wish my intermediary had done a better job when he approached my son's adoptive family by offering them counselling. Three years after the reunion my son's mother went ahead and got some counselling for herself. Adoptive parents do suffer in silence when adopted children and their birth families are in touch with each other. I am sure that if all parties of the adoption triangle received counselling at this crucial time a lot of questions could be answered, which would mean a little less heartache.

Knowing both sides of the coin

I gave up my son for adoption almost 18 years ago, and subsequently became an adoptive parent myself. I now have an adopted son who is eight years old and I feel I have an unusual angle on things, as I have personal experience of two sides of the adoption triangle. I think that my own feelings for my natural son have helped to answer some of my adopted son's questions about whether or not his natural mother and other relatives still think and care about him. I am fortunate enough to have a fairly open relationship with my adopted son's natural family, albeit through the adoption society, but the exchange of cards, letters and photos has been helpful for both families. I would have welcomed such openness after my natural son was adopted, but the situation was very different then.

Many adoptive parents say that they don't welcome open adoptions because they feel it would minimise their role as parents and lead to confusion for the child. In my experience, the reverse has proved to be the case. I do not feel threatened by the fact that my adopted son's natural family know all about me and my family. On the contrary, I know that they feel reassured and relaxed knowing he is being cared for and brought up in a loving home. (If only I had that reassurance from my natural son's adoptive family!) As for my adopted son, he knows his natural family cares for him and understands, as much as an eight-year-old can, the reasons for his adoption. He expresses a desire to trace his natural family when he is older and I am more than happy to assist him in this. I don't feel that this undermines my parenthood, but feel that by being able to talk freely about his feelings, needs and wishes for the future, my adopted son can grow up well adjusted and secure in the knowledge that he is a very well-loved child.

My natural son is never far from my thoughts and my adopted younger son has not in any way replaced him, as I'm sure subsequent children for other birth mothers do not replace their lost children. However, I feel more relaxed talking about him now, especially with my adopted son, who I feel can understand some of the mixed feelings involved.

CHAPTER 16

The Adoptee's Story

Coming to terms with being adopted is a challenge that faces every adoptee, however loving and secure the adoptive home they are brought into and raised in. It is seldom easy and for some it is a daily challenge that can haunt them consciously or subconsciously.

Some see their adoptive family as a safe haven; others wonder what life would have been like with their birth families. Many have to deal at an early age with the sort of deep emotional pain that most born-to children don't experience until they are much older.

However hard it is for birth and adoptive parents, it is hardest of all for the adoptee, who is powerless and often without choice in the many decisions that are made for them.

In this chapter adoptees tell their side of the story.

• • •

I don't know anything

I don't know anything, really, about my natural parents, and that upsets me a lot. It's hard to know the difference between what I remember and what I've been told. Sometimes I make up stories about my early childhood, about those first 13 months, because I just desperately want to have a part of my life that's entirely mine, my very own. Being adopted, I often feel that everything I've got, including my name, has been given to me by my adoptive parents. I need to feel that I came to my parents with something that was already mine.

Room for one more

I am ten and a half years old. I have two sisters, who are eight and seven. We became part of our 'forever family' nearly four years ago and were legally adopted on mum's birthday two years ago.

One thing that I think is very important to adopted children is their life story book. I often look at mine with mum and dad and it helps me to remember the good times as well as the bad times. My foster mum and dad were also very important to me. Mum and dad have become good friends with them and we usually visit them in Coventry at least once a year. They come to see us when they are on holiday near our home, bringing with them the children they are caring for at the time.

We are all very excited now because we are adopting another little girl who is three and a half years old. She came to live with our family in June. Mum and dad actually heard about her from a *Be My Parent* news-sheet last December, although we have recently seen her picture in last August's issue of the *Adoption UK Journal*, which came out before mum and dad started taking it.

My new sister is very good and is learning very quickly despite having learning difficulties, although mum says this could be the 'honeymoon' period!

Before we had her, mum and dad had to go through a lot of visits from social workers to make sure we were the right family. We were all included in the visits, because it had to be right for my sisters and me as well. It made me realise what mum and dad had to go through before they became our parents. It is nice having a little sister again because I was used to looking after little ones in the past. Mum tells me not to feel responsible for her, just enjoy her, but I do feel it comes naturally to me and can't help it sometimes.

We all went to meet our new sister because it had to be right for all of us. From the first meeting to the second it took five weeks, which seemed for ever to us, but it gave mum and dad a chance to get everything ready. We spent four days with her, taking her out and about before bringing her home with us on the train, which took about eight hours. All of us, including my new sister, are now getting back to everyday life, and as I have said – so far, so good. We all seem to do different things with her. I like to watch over her and help her with anything she finds difficult. One of my sisters is very gentle with her and the other likes to rough and tumble with her and has found another tomboy like herself!

A selection of adoptees' poems

Reassurance

I open my mouth but no words come out,
I reach out but I can't touch you,
I feel trapped, caged, frustrated.

You don't know how I feel,
You never felt the pain,
You never cried to sleep,
You never hated as I did,
You were never hated as I was.

But still you open the door,
And let the sunshine stream through.
You take me in your arms and cradle me,
You stroke my hair and reassure me,
Because you love me.

Nightmare

I wake up,
The tears are still hot on my face,
I saw her,
I felt her pain,
I screamed her anguish,
I bled her blood,
But I couldn't protect her,
I was just as helpless as her.

I wake up,
My head is still pounding,
Then I realise,
The pain was mine,
The anguish was mine,
The blood was mine,
I couldn't protect her,
I was helpless.
It was me,
My pain,
My anguish,
My blood,
My broken life still haunting me.
As I cry I shut my eyes,
Why me, why?

By Astra (aged 15)

Leaving home

You're leaving home, all those familiar faces.
You say goodbye and off you go.
You arrive somewhere strange – strange faces.
You're left alone.
You want your family that you know.
Then finally you can go and see them.
You're having a great time but you're taken away again.
I ask my mum and dad: 'When will I come back?'
They say they are not sure.
'You may get a new family.'
I don't need a new one – I've got my own.
My face came in a magazine.
They say they've found a family.

Goodbye again – but this time it is for good.
My new family want me very much.
I suppose they're very nice,
so perhaps I will get used to living here.

By Caroline (aged 10)

Caroline is a birth child of this family. She wrote this reflecting on the experiences of her adoptive and foster siblings.

Born in the heart

I am a second-year social care student and I am adopted. I have chosen to do my assessment project for my course on adoption and I think that the experiences I would like to share as an adoptee are: that anyone adopting a child should treat that child just the same as any 'natural' children they might have, as my parents have always done; and that they should tell the adopted child about their adoption from an early age, as my parents have done. If the child remains uninformed until the later years it can cause so much upset and bitterness. This happened in my fiancé's case. He was not told of his adoption until he was 15 and in the middle of a heated argument. This caused him to leave home and the relationship with his parents is now very strained.

I would also recommend that adoptive parents do not try to discourage their children from finding out about and seeking their natural parents if they wish to do so. It is not a rejection of them if the child chooses to seek his or her 'natural' parents; it is only the completion of a picture of themselves. Really, it is mainly curiosity.

Finally, I would just like to recount something a GP said when my mum adopted me and which I think sums up what adoption means perfectly. He said: 'Although the child isn't born in your womb, she is born in your heart.' In my case this is true: I am as much theirs as my two brothers, who are their 'natural' children.

When I was eight years old…

I was adopted, now I am 12. I used to go to a special school by bus every day. I didn't like it because people cussed me for going there. I could not read or write and I was naughty. I was naughty a lot.

Two years ago I went to mainstream school. I did Year 5 twice so I could catch up. My first helper was Jenny but she had a baby. I have Sue now. Now I take Ritalin and I am good some of the time.

Sometimes I get angry and I get into trouble. But now I know all my times tables and I can read Goose Bumps books. I am good at spelling. I am a good swimmer and I have been in a lot of swimming galas. Last year I got a silver medal in the London youth games. I like sailing and I am doing my Level 3 RYA badge. On 13 March I went to the civic centre to get an award from the Mayor of Southwark. Only 60 people got the award. It was for achievement. Because I have done so well I got a £5 book token, a plaque and a T-shirt saying, 'I am an achiever.'

Adoption day

On 24 March, it was my, Maria's and Catriona's adoption day. We are eight, seven and five years old. We all have been living with mum and dad for three years.

In the morning I felt very embarrassed but also very, very happy. When we went downstairs to have breakfast we saw presents on the table, all wrapped up. When I opened my present I saw it was a watch. I jumped up from the table and hugged my mum and dad to say thank you.

We drove to the court to see the judge. We could not find a parking place and thought we would be late. We had some flowers to give to our social workers and our solicitor. We picked the flowers from our garden. We went to see the judge, called Marian. She showed us our certificates and told us we are the Grange family, not the James family any more. She showed us where mummy and daddy had signed. Then we signed our own certificates and each other's. We did this to show that we are one whole family. I felt very happy after this.

On the way out we saw four people with wigs on; they looked very funny. Later on that day we went to have lunch at Piccolo's. Lunch was very nice. The people in Piccolo's were very jolly, too. They are Italian. They had made a cake for us which was chocolate with our names in cream. I blew a party popper at a man who was eating spaghetti and he jumped, but didn't mind.

When we got home we got presents from granny and mum and dad. I had a china tea set. Maria had a china doll. Catriona had a lovely old bear called Edward. All of them have been passed on from our family and are over one-hundred years old.

Our rector came round for some prayers for our adoption in our house. Mummy and daddy said a prayer together. Then we had some cake! When he had gone we had tea and went to bed early because we were all so happy and exhausted.

My story

I have moved to lots of places and I've had four mums as well as foster parents. It felt so horrible. I have been to five schools, which was really horrible. I am living in Cirencester now, which is a nice place. I have got a mum and sister. My sister is called Abby and is nearly six years old. I have a mum called Sarah who is 33 years old. My mum first saw a picture of me in the *Adoption UK Journal* last August.

Since moving into my forever family I have gone through a lot of changes. I am doing very well at my private school. I have got so many best friends and I have got on with people.

By Amanda Pollard (aged 11)

My adoption

In the year of 1988 my mum and dad had a baby called Sara. It was me. The next year my brother Matthew was born. I thought he was very cute. A few months later my mum and dad decided to move to France for a year.

After we had got back to England a social worker called Julie and some friends came to our house and said, 'You are not looking after your children properly so I have to take them to our offices to be looked after by someone else till they can be adopted.' They took us into the dark, cold night. My feet were more cold than yours would be because I was only in my nightie and was wearing slippers rather than shoes. A man gave me and Matthew some Polos when we were going to the car and drove us to some buildings. These were the offices. When we were inside they looked for some people to look after us for the night.

The next day the social workers came to us and said, 'Now we're going to take you to Sandra and Mick.' So we got into the car. When we got there Sandra and Mick were waiting for us. I said: 'Hello.' I had a lovely time; so did Matthew. You would too, I hope.

Now let's get back to the story. After a year, Julie came back. 'We are taking you to Steve and Diane, your new foster parents,' she said. We thought they were nicer than Sandra and Mick. That's when I started school. I really enjoyed it. Every so often some people called Anna and Dave came to visit us. They were going to be our new proper parents. After two years we were adopted. To be adopted you have to see the judge, and ours even allowed us to change our names.

Feelings: I've felt happy, sad, frightened, nervous and scared.

By Sara (aged 8)

An important message

When I was five or four I had lost all my family and it is very bad when I think of my family. It was sad to move to England. I had to go on an airplane when I was little and I went to Heathrow and then had to go to a children's home. I used to live in the children's home and next I was lucky to have a nice family who live in England. I have got a mum and dad and two brothers and one sister and the puss. It's nice to play with them and you can share things. You can be happy with your father and mother and sister and brother and they will help you a lot and you need to know how to help them. Now I've got a good family and I am very happy. Family is a good thing.

I'm jealous

I'm envious of kids who aren't adopted and who have natural parents – especially when they look like them. And I'm jealous because there are times when I think my original parents might be nicer than the ones I have now. I'm not saying my parents aren't nice, because they are, but maybe my other parents wouldn't be so strict.

My interesting life

As a roaring fire proceeded to consume the big hotel on the end of our street, I ran back to our lodgings, squealing with delight at something I had never seen before. Later that night, my sister, aged nine, and I, aged five, would be picked up in an ambulance and taken away from my mother (displaying similar symptoms to that of the raging fire). This would be the beginning of what at the time I thought was an adventure but I now look on as a struggle to reach a better life.

From then on I stuck to my sister like dung to a blanket (much to her dislike) as we progressed from care worker to care worker.

Boasting has always been great for attracting attention, something I tried to do frequently as a child, and this rather dramatic story, along with a full description of exactly what nationality I am, always seemed to turn heads. Rather a cheeky, rude and slow child, I annoyed many people and was difficult to live with. My foster parents discovered this and often tired of my constant demands for attention while there were three other children to attend to in the house. For the three years Emma and I lived with our foster family we had lots of fun, opportunities, holidays in Wales and the good care we needed.

Once a family was found for us, my sister thought how hard it would be to leave the happy life we had lived with our foster family, but I ran around the playground showing all my friends photos of my new big brother and sister. Looking back I regret the fact that I didn't shed a tear as I left for my new home. Maybe I should have showed some gratitude for what they had done for me.

I settled in straight away and made new friends at school, improved in my work and received more attention from my new parents, who had more time. Two years later, aged ten, I would be adopted into a happy family life. That was the end of all the social workers who didn't really help. I owe a big 'thank you' to Barnardos though, and look back with nostalgia at the life scrapbook I made with a social worker there.

Through those first years with my new family I developed a lot in mental ability and maturity, and became less attention seeking. We all enjoyed our long caravanning holidays. Some of my favourite occupations were gardening with my dad and swimming and cooking with my mum. At school I progressed really well.

Now I'm doing my GCSEs and you could say that my sister (who is at university after A, B and C grades at A-level) and I are two of the success stories of the care system. I have a good future ahead of me.

By Gillian (aged 14)

Where I came from, where I belong

My adoptive mother and I haven't always got on, but as I've grown older and a bit wiser we've become closer and closer, until now I would say she's my best friend and the best mother I could wish for. Friends of mine who have grown up with their natural parents actually envy my relationship with her, which I find somewhat amusing given my adoptive status. My mum has always been very encouraging about me finding my birth mother; she was once a social worker and a guardian *ad litem*, and has a good inside knowledge of the kinds of benefits it can bring to an adopted person. I was a difficult child, and I now realise that this was at least partly because I hadn't come to terms with being adopted.

My mother's encouragement led me to make a fundamental mistake when carrying out my search for my birth mother, which I undertook between the ages of 18 and 25. I thought that because mum was so positive about it she was feeling okay about the whole thing – so I didn't take the time and effort to think through exactly what she might be feeling when I told her I was meeting my birth mother in a month's time. You can imagine how shocked I was when her first reaction was to burst into tears.

Her second reaction, which utterly horrified me, was to say, 'It's alright if you want to go back to her now, I understand, she's your real mother. I won't stand in your way.' It still breaks my heart to know that she could even think that I might want to do that. My mum is my real mother, and it was only then that I realised that she didn't, in her heart of hearts, quite trust that I saw it that way.

I have tried many times, without success, to describe exactly how my adoptive mother and my birth mother both fit into my life. The closest I can get is that my birth mother represents my roots: she is where I come from, where I get my blue eyes and big feet from. She created me: without her I wouldn't exist – literally. That means she's very special to me. One of the things my mum found most difficult to cope with was that I wanted to carry on seeing my birth mother after I'd made contact with her; she thought, I suppose, that once I had found my roots I would be happy and 'return' to my old life. Well, finding your roots for the first time in your life changes you for ever, and once you've made contact with that essential jigsaw piece, the last thing you want to do is to let it go again. I get on very well with my birth mother, and I'm constantly finding out more about her that fits in with my own character and background. She's my only link with the person I was born as. Like any relationship, it's an ongoing process, and not one I always feel happy with: I feel, for example, that she still treats me as if I'm the baby she let go rather than respecting me as an adult and a full human being. She rarely takes an interest in my life or asks about what I'm doing. But I persevere because what she means to me is far more valuable than whether or not she asks me how my work's going.

I sometimes think my mum, on the other hand, knows more about me than I do myself! Whereas my birth mother is where I come from, my adoptive mother is where I belong. If what mum had expected to happen had happened and I had gone to my birth mother's family, then as far as I'm concerned it would have been like losing my family all over again. Finding your roots is not finding another family – that's something which I think my adoptive mother still doesn't quite understand or accept. It would make life an awful lot easier for her if she did. Once I lost my birth family they were lost to me for good. By the time I found the family I had when I was a baby they were no longer my family. This whole process gives you a lot of insight into what families and parenthood are all about, and I know now that families are made because they go through the bad times as well as the good times together, and help each other and have rows over a period of years and years, a whole lifetime in fact. I haven't been through any bad times with my birth family and probably won't. That's precisely why they'll never be my family. In fact, one of the ironies about finding my birth mother is that it's finally made me realise that where I belong is in my adoptive family, despite a childhood of suspecting that I didn't because I was adopted.

After a very rocky and very scary time when I thought for a while I was going to lose my mum (and both of us, it later emerged, went through a grieving process very similar to losing a parent or a child), I think we've finally worked it out, and as a result of the things we were forced to say at that time we've become even closer. I see my birth mother less often, partly in sympathy for mum's feelings, but also because I've come to realise that it is an uneven relationship and I need some space from it. There is no blueprint for a relationship with a birth mother, and I find myself floundering about and making mistakes all over the place. She's not just a friend, and she is important – but not as important as my own family. I usually give up trying to talk about it as I can't even describe it to myself, let alone anyone else.

One conclusion that I have come to is this: it's impossible for me to understand exactly what either my adoptive mother or my birth mother is going through. Although I can make a guess, I haven't been through it myself. In a similar way, I don't think my adoptive mum will ever understand quite what it's like to be an adopted person. Why should she? She's always been able to take it for granted that the family she sees around her are her genetic roots. I, on the other hand, never knew who I really was or where I really came from until I met my birth mother: that – and only that (although it's pretty fundamental) – is her importance to me.

Well-Known Adopters and Adoptees, Past and Present

Hundreds of children are adopted every year and their adoptive parents come from all walks of life. Here are the names of just a few of the better known adoptive parents:

David Bellamy, botanist writer and broadcaster
Dora Bryan, actor
Jilly Cooper, writer
Tom Cruise and Nicole Kidman, actors
Mia Farrow and Andre Previn, actress and conductor
Jeremy Hardy, comedian
Lenny Henry and Dawn French, comedians
Will Hutton, editor of *The Observer*
Kiri te Kanawa, New Zealand opera singer – she is also an adoptee
Penelope Keith, actress
Joan Lester, former MP
Bob Monkhouse, comedian
Baroness Nicholson of Winterbourne, former MP
Duke and Duchess of Richmond (Goodwood House)
Lord David Steele, former leader of the Liberal Democrats
Lord Wakeham, former Lord Privy Seal and Leader of the House of Lords
Dennis Waterman and Rula Lenska, actors

…And did you know that the following people where not brought up by their birth parents and were either adopted, fostered or spent many of their early years in a children's home?

Kate Adie, journalist and television correspondent, famous for her reports from war zones. Her mother became pregnant while her husband was away at war and Kate was adopted as a baby. She has recently traced and met her birth family.

Jim Bowen, British comedian and host of the TV quiz game *Bullseye*. He was adopted as a baby.

Richard Burton, Welsh actor. Burton was born the youngest of 13 children in a poor mining family in South Wales. His mother died when he was quite young and he was then raised by his sister. Later, he was fostered by his teacher, Philip Burton, who, too close in age to be able to adopt him, became Richard Burton's legal guardian and gave him his surname.

Truman Capote, American author. At the age of six his parents abandoned him to the care of some elderly maternal cousins: three sisters and a brother, all unmarried and living together.

Gabrielle (Coco) Chanel, French fashion designer. Orphaned at the age of six, she opened her first shop in Deauville in 1913. She became the queen of Paris haute couture and remained one of the most influential French designers for six decades.

Sydney and Sir Charles (Charlie) Chaplin, British-American actors. From the ages of six and two, the boys never had a stable home with two parents and spent most of the time in the workhouse, orphanages and on the streets.

George Cole, British actor (Arthur Daley in *Minder*). He was fostered as a baby but did not find out until he was 13. When his foster father died he was adopted by actor Alastair Sim and his wife.

Dame Catherine Cookson, author. Catherine Cookson was born to a young unmarried woman and raised by her grandparents. Until she was seven she thought that her mother was her older sister; finding out that she was illegitimate was a lasting shock, leading to a nervous breakdown in her thirties. She went on to become one of the most successful novelists of historical romances of all time.

Shirley Ann Field, British actress. Evacuated to the north of England during World War II and then sent to a children's home. She had almost no contact with her family from then on.

Ella Fitzgerald, black American jazz singer. Both of Ella's parents died when she was a young child and she was brought up in an orphanage until the age of 15. She was 'discovered' by Chick Webb, who was looking for a new singer, and he and his wife then fostered her.

Sam Goldwyn, American film producer and one of the owners of MGM studios. Goldwyn was born Samuel Gelbfisz in the infamous Warsaw Ghetto. His parents had both died by the time he was 11. He emigrated first to England in 1899 and then to the USA. He became one of the most powerful men in the film industry.

Larry Grayson, comedian and gameshow host. He was born William White to an unmarried working-class girl and a coal miner in Nuneaton. His adoptive foster mother died when he was six, he was raised by his much older adoptive foster sisters.

Eric Hobsbawm, British historian. A German-Jewish refugee, he came to Britain in the 1930s. By the time he was 14 both his parents had died. Educated at Cambridge, he is recognised as one of Britain's foremost historians.

Anthony Hopkins, musician, writer and broadcaster. Adopted at the age of three or four.

Jane Lapotaire, British actress. Long-term foster child.

Naomi Marsh, actress and patron of Talkadoption. She is the adopted daughter of the Duke and Duchess of Richmond.

Brian Moore, rugby player. Moore was adopted as a baby. He has been capped 63 times for England – more than any other player. He has also been Captain of the English Rugby Team.

Eric Morley, entertainment entrepreneur. Morley was orphaned at the age of 11 and sent to a naval training ship. He has become an entertainment and media tycoon.

Bruce Oldfield, fashion designer. Brought up in a Barnardo's home after being abandoned as a baby.

Edgar Allan Poe, American poet and short-story writer. His parents died before he was six and he was raised by a merchant named John Allan. By the time he was six the family had moved to England, but he was back in America by the age of 11.

Edgar Wallace, thriller writer. Wallace was born to an unmarried woman and fostered by a Billingsgate fish porter and his wife, who already had ten children, when he was nine days old. He became a successful and widely read author.

Phillip Whitehead, writer and television producer, chairman of the Consumers' Association and Member of Parliament 1970–1983.

Terry Wiles, a thalidomide baby and transracial adoptee. His life story was made famous in the book *On Giant's Shoulders.*

These are just a handful of the thousands of people who have been brought up by adoptive or foster parents and have made a success of their lives.

Adoption: A Legal Outline

By Richard White

(Richard White of White & Sherwin is a solicitor with a specialist knowledge of adoption law and is a member of Adoption UK.)

Introduction

This article provides an outline of the law affecting the placement of children for adoption and the subsequent legal proceedings. Readers must remember that there may be major changes to adoption law, though they are now unlikely to take effect before 2001. The detail may also vary, because there may be more minor legal changes and because practice in your local area may differ. If your case is of any complexity or you are dissatisfied with the advice you are getting, consider seeking the advice of a solicitor experienced in adoption work.

In general terms there are three types of adoption:

1. Agency placement, where an adoption agency carries out its duties to find a family for a child

2. In family, application by step-parent or relative

3. Private application, by private foster parent or intercountry adoption.

What follows is approached from the viewpoint of agency placements, which are the most common, but it can also be applied to the other categories as appropriate.

Comprehensive adoption service

Every local authority must establish and maintain within their area a service designed to meet the needs, in relation to adoption, of

(a) children who have been or may be adopted

(b) parents and guardians of such children

(c) persons who have adopted or may adopt a child, and for that purpose must provide the requisite facilities themselves or through a voluntary adoption society.

Adoption agencies must appoint an adoption panel, which has to consider and make recommendations on

(a) whether adoption is in the best interests of the child, and if so, whether a freeing application under 18 should be made

(b) whether a prospective adopter is suitable to be an adoptive parent

(c) whether a prospective adopter is suitable for a particular child.

It is the panel which recommends and the agency which must reach a decision, having considered the recommendation. The duty laid down in the Adoption Act states:

In reaching any decision relating to the adoption of a child, a court or adoption agency shall have regard to all the circumstances, first consideration being given to the need to safeguard and promote the welfare of the child throughout his childhood; and shall so far as practicable ascertain the wishes or feelings of the child regarding the decision and give due consideration to them, having regard to his age and understanding.

Who may be adopted?

The child must be under 18 at the time of the order, single and never have been married. An order can still be made even if only a short period of childhood remains. Where

(a) an applicant is a parent, step-parent or relative of the child, or

(b) the child was placed with the applicant(s) by an adoption agency or by order of the High Court.

An adoption order shall not be made until the child is at least 19 weeks old and at all times during the preceding 13 weeks has had his home with the applicants or one of them. In any other case the child must be at least 12 months old and have had his home with the applicants or one of them at all times from the 12 months before the order is made.

The effect of adoption

An adoption order is an irrevocable court order vesting parental responsibility relating to a child in the adopters. The order extinguishes the legal relationship between the child and the birth parents.

Where the adopters are a married couple, an adopted child shall be treated in law as if he had been born as a child of the marriage, whether or not he was in fact born after the marriage was solemnised. An adopted child shall be treated in law as if he were not the child of any person other than the adopters or adopter.

The court making the adoption order will send a copy of the order to the General Register Office, who will then send the adopters an adoption certificate, which replaces the child's birth certificate.

Although the adopters can choose not to change the child's surname, it is normally changed to that of the adopters on the making of the adoption order. The adoption application provides for the new names to be identified, and these will be shown on the adoption order and the adoption certificate. These documents are not normally seen by the birth family.

An adoption order made in the United Kingdom confers British citizenship, provided at least one of the applicants is a British citizen. A child born in the United Kingdom since 1 January 1983 is not automatically British, so consideration should always be given to whether the effect of the adoption order will be to acquire citizenship for the child.

Who may apply?

An adoption order may be made on the application of a married couple where each has attained the age of 21 years, or 18 where that person is the father or mother of the child, provided that person's spouse has attained the age of 21. An adoption order may be made on the application of one person, where he has attained the age of 21 years, and he or she is either not married, or if married, the court is satisfied that the spouse cannot be found, or the parties have separated and are living apart and the separation is likely to be permanent, or the spouse is incapable of making an application for an adoption order by reason of physical or mental ill health.

There is no specific upper age limit, though most agencies are unlikely to place a younger child with older applicants, unless there are special reasons. You should check if the agency to which you are applying has a specific policy.

An application may not be made by an unmarried couple. An application for adoption could be made by one of them. The other could then obtain parental responsibility under a residence order.

Applicants for adoption or one of them must be domiciled in the United Kingdom, the Channel Islands or the Isle of Man. If neither applicant is domiciled in this country, application may be made for a proposed foreign adoption order, which gives permission for the child to be taken out of the country to be adopted elsewhere. Domicile is a complex subject, and if you have any doubt about your status, you should check with a solicitor or ask your agency to do so.

Race and culture

A local authority has a duty to any child it is looking after to give due consideration, in making any decision about the child, to the child's religious persuasion, racial origin and cultural and linguistic background.

Removal of child from placement

Experience shows that many of those working with children are not familiar with the following provisions, so they should be considered carefully, if there are problems with the placement.

Before application to the court

A child may not be removed from a person with whom he has his home by the adoption agency, unless it has given seven days notice of intention to remove. If the child has been living with the applicant for five years, the consent of the court is required for removal against the will of the prospective adopter, if notice of intention to adopt has been given to the authority where the applicant lives within the last three months.

After application to the court

Where an adoption application has been filed, the placing agency cannot remove the child, unless the court gives consent for the agency to serve its notice of intention to remove. Where an application has been filed and a parent or guardian has agreed to the making of the adoption order, a child may not be removed by that parent or guardian from the person with whom he has his home, without the consent of the court. If a parent changes their mind, seek legal advice quickly.

One consequence of these provisions is that foster parents who do not have the support of the care authority to adopt may still be able to apply for an adoption order. Where they give notice of their intention to apply for adoption and make an application to the court, the child may not be removed by the local authority without the leave of the court. Foster parents should not exercise this power, unless there is a genuine prospect of them making a successful application.

Application to the court

Applications for adoption or for a freeing order may be made to the family proceedings' court, any divorce county court, or the High Court in London. Most applications are made in the county court. You can obtain an application form from the court or solicitors.

Once the application has been filed at court, a court officer is required to list the case for hearing as soon as practicable after the originating process has been filed. In practice, county courts usually issue a notice stating that the hearing will take place on a date to be fixed and that directions may be given. The court will then appoint a reporting officer or guardian *ad litem* depending on the nature of the application. The hearing will be fixed when their reports have been filed and the judge has considered them. In the county court practice thereafter varies; if those whose agreement to the order is required have given their agreement, the court will fix a hearing date, which will not be notified to the parent.

Serial number application

On an adoption application applicants who wish to keep their identity confidential may apply for a serial number. The court assigns it and must ensure that the proceedings are conducted with a view to maintaining that anonymity.

Applications which are not agreed

The application form requires the applicant to state whether the parents or guardian agree to the making of an adoption order. In those cases where agreement is not given, the applicants must file a statement in triplicate of the facts on which they intend to rely in support of their application to dispense with the parents' agreement. Where agreement has been withdrawn after the making of the application, the applicants must then file notice of the application to dispense with agreement and the statement of facts.

If a parent does not agree to the making of an adoption order, the prospective adopters will have to include a statement of facts with their application to the court. This should be drafted by a person who understands the relevant law, since it will set out the case on which the court can decide to dispense with the agreement of the parent.

Schedule 2 report

After the prospective adopters have filed their application in court, the placing agency, or in the case of a step-parent application or private placement, the local authority where the child resides, must file a Schedule 2 report (so-called because it is Schedule 2 to the Rules of Court). This sets out details of the applicants, the child, the birth parents and the work which the agency has undertaken. The filing of the Schedule 2 report can be a source of delay in some authorities. Little progress can be made until the report has been filed, so press your social worker for a time limit.

Appointment and role of court officers

For the purpose of any application for an adoption order or a freeing order, there may be appointed a reporting officer or guardian *ad litem*. They are appointed by the court from panels established by, but independent of, local authorities.

Reporting officer

If the application is agreed the court will appoint a reporting officer, whose duties are to:

(a) ensure so far as is reasonably practicable that any agreement to the making of the adoption order is govern freely and unconditionally and with full understanding of what is involved

(b) witness the signature by parent or guardian of the written agreement to the making of the adoption order

(c) investigate circumstances relevant to the agreement

(d) report to the court in writing, drawing attention to any matters which may assist the court.

Guardian ad litem

A guardian *ad litem* will be appointed to carry out duties on behalf of the child if the case is contested or complex, or if the application is made in the High Court. The duties are to investigate the application, the Schedule 2 report, any statement of facts and any other matters considered relevant.

In the case of a High Court application, the Official Solicitor may be appointed as guardian of the child. Unless the case is particularly complex, it is increasingly common to appoint a panel guardian, who must instruct a solicitor to act for the child.

Disclosure of reports

Reports to the court are normally regarded as confidential but they may be disclosed in certain circumstances. They may be disclosed with parts made anonymous. Prospective adopters should ensure that they know what parts of a report are being disclosed, and that they are content with what is disclosed. While there should not be unnecessary secrecy in adoption proceedings, the courts do seek to ensure that disclosure of information is in the interests of the child.

Conduct of hearing

In the case of a contested application, the court must consider the totality of the evidence. If satisfied that adoption is for the child's welfare, the court should then ask itself whether there are grounds for dispensation of the agreement of the parent.

If the application is not agreed, the parents will be given notice to attend to put their case, and, in the case of a serial number application, the applicants will be required to attend at another time not notified to the parents. The order in which they are heard may depend on the circumstances of the case and local practice.

In the High Court and some county courts there are facilities for all parties to be present at court at the same time without meeting. Arrangements should be made carefully with the court and between solicitors to ensure that parties do not meet accidentally.

Attendance at court

The judge shall not make an adoption order except after the personal attendance of the applicants and the child before him, unless, in special circumstances the court directs otherwise. In the High Court a direction is often given that the child need not attend, but the applicants may still request the judge to see the child once the order is made.

Agreement to adoption

An adoption order cannot be made unless

(a) the child is free for adoption; or

(b) in the case of each parent or guardian of the child the court is satisfied that

(i) he freely, and with full understanding of what is involved, agrees unconditionally to the making of an adoption order; or

(ii) his agreement to the making of the adoption order should be dispensed with.

The agreement of the mother to a freeing order or an adoption order is ineffective, if given less than six weeks after the birth of the child. The agreement may not be made conditional on, for example, the adopter agreeing to contact between child and birth parent, though there may be negotiations between the parties.

Whose agreement?

The agreement required is that of each parent or guardian. 'Parent' means in relation to a child, a parent who has parental responsibility for the child. An unmarried father is not qualified as a parent, unless he has parental responsibility by agreement with the mother or by court order.

Dispensing with parental agreement

The court has to be satisfied that there are grounds for dispensing with the agreement of a parent or guardian. These are that the parent or guardian

(a) cannot be found (in the case of missing parents) or is incapable of giving agreement (in the case of mentally ill parents)

(b) is withholding his agreement unreasonably

(c) has persistently failed without reasonable cause to discharge his parental responsibility for the child

(d) has abandoned or neglected the child

(e) has persistently ill-treated the child

(f) has seriously ill-treated the child (provided also that the rehabilitation or the child within the household of the parent of guardian is unlikely).

The most commonly used ground is that the parent is 'withholding his agreement unreasonably'. The court has to be satisfied, not that the parent is blameworthy or that the court believes adoption is in the interests of the child, but that the parent is unreasonable. The court will weigh up all the facts, including that a reasonable parent pays regard to the welfare of his child.

Freeing for adoption

A freeing order enables the issue of parental agreement to be resolved before the child is placed for adoption or before applicants seeks an adoption order. This has the benefit that the child can be placed in the knowledge that conflict over the agreement has been dealt with. In practice there may be disadvantages for the child and for adopters, in dealing with the matter in proceedings to which the adopters are not parties. A freeing application may also cause delay in the placement of the child. In general, if the child is living with prospective adopters, an adoption application may be preferable to a freeing application.

Adoption or residence order

It is sometimes suggested that the court should make a residence order rather than an adoption order. The main differences are:

(a) an adoption order vests parental responsibility in adopters and extinguishes the parental responsibility of the birth parents

and

(b) a residence order may be discharged and ends automatically when the child is 16, or in exceptional circumstances, 18, whereas the effects of an adoption order are lifelong; birth parents retain parental responsibility and status to be shared with the adopters.

Adoption and finance

Payment of money in connection with adoption is in principle unlawful, but the court may approve payments in certain circumstances. If a payment is made which is not approved, there is an absolute bar to the making of an adoption order.

Adoption allowances

Provisions prohibiting the payment of money do not apply to any payment made as an adoption allowance. Allowances are normally only paid by local authority adoption agencies. The rate is usually related to a fostering allowance but this depends on the individual agency.

A decision about payment of an allowance must be taken before an adoption order is made. Consideration should always be given to whether an allowance should be paid in principle even though initially on a nil basis, in case the adopters' circumstances change after the adoption. Any allowance paid under the regulations must be reviewed at least annually and could be decreased.

FINANCIAL TRAPS

Adopters become financially liable for the child on the making of an adoption order. There is a breakdown rate in adoption, especially with older children. If the local authority has to take over the accommodation of an adopted child, the authority will look to the adopters for contributions to the maintenance of the child. Local authority policies vary but they are often unsympathetic to the idea that the adopters originally adopted as a service to the child. Having an allowance may offer some protection against large bills.

SOCIAL SECURITY AND TAX

Child benefit is payable for the child from the time of placement for adoption. Income tax is not payable on an adoption allowance provided it does not contain any element of profit.

Adoption and contact

A local authority has a duty to allow a child in its care reasonable contact with his parents or guardian, and to endeavour to promote contact, unless it is not reasonably practicable or consistent with the welfare of the child, between the child and his parents, any other person with parental responsibility and others connected with him. If the local authority decides to place the child for adoption it will have to consider how to deal with contact, whether by reduction by agreement or court order or by termination by court order.

The 1989 Act gave an impetus to thinking about the kind of contact which may be appropriate and the type of case in which some form of contact or information giving is suitable. This may be direct, physical contact or indirect contact, perhaps through a letter box service provided by an adoption agency.

The courts have said that they have power to make a contact order be effective after an adoption order. An application may be heard at the same time as the adoption application or, with the prior consent of the court, after the order has been made. Courts are, however, reluctant to impose orders on unwilling adopters and prefer to leave questions of contact to the adopters. They may require the adopters to justify their wishes in relation to contact.

Adopters should be advised to consider carefully a number of balancing factors:

1. Will the proposed form of contact lead to the disclosure of information, including the whereabouts of the child, which the adopters would prefer to withhold?

2. How will the child view the proposed form of contact?

3. Will the proposed form of contact undermine the relationship of child and adopters or will it be supportive to the placement?

4. Will the proposed form of contact promote the long term welfare of the adoptee?

5. Do the risks associated with the proposed form of contact, especially given the characteristics of the person with whom it is proposed to have contact, outweigh its possible benefit to the child in the long-term?

If at the time of the making of the adoption order the adopters had indicated their willingness to follow a certain course of action in relation to contact (it would seem whether direct or indirect), and they later changed their minds, they should expect to have to give their reasons for doing so. If they did not do so, an applicant seeking leave to apply for an order might well be given consent to make an application. The birth parent would still have to make out a strong case to justify a fresh order.

Indirect contact

Prospective adopters are now frequently advised that they should be prepared to provide photographs and/or reports about the child's progress to interested members of the birth family via the adoption agency. Each case must still be considered individually.

APPENDIX 3

Useful Organisations

British adoption organisations

Adoption UK
Lower Boddington
Daventry, Northamptonshire NN11 6YB
Tel: 01327 260295 Email: adoption@adoptionuk.org.uk
(Supporting adoptive families before, during and after adoption.)

BAAFLINK
MEA House
Ellison Place, Newcastle upon Tyne NE1 8XS
Tel: 0191 261 6600 Email: newcastle@baaf.org.uk

Be My Parent (BMP)
200 Union Street, London SE1 0LX
Tel: 0171 593 2060/1/2/3 Email: bmp@baaf.org.uk
(Photo listing service of children needing new families.)

British Agencies for Adoption and Fostering (BAAF)
Head Office, Skyline House
200 Union Street, London SE1 0LX
Tel: 0171 593 2000 Email: mail@baaf.org.uk

(BAAF is an umbrella group for professionals and agencies involved in adoption. BAAF can provide a list of all current registered adoption agencies. There are local BAAF offices in Edinburgh, Cardiff, Birmingham, Leeds, Newcastle upon Tyne and Bristol.)

Children's Legal Centre
University of Essex, Wivenhoe Park
Colchester, Essex CO4 3SQ
Tel: 01206 872466 Email: clc@essex.ac.uk

Contact a Family
107 Tottenham Court Road
London W1P 0HA
Tel: 0171 383 3555 Email: information@cafamily.org.uk
(Helps families caring for children with any disability or special need.)

Family Rights Group
Print House
18 Ashwin Street, London E8 3DL
Tel: 0171 923 2628 Email: office@frg.u-net.com
(National charity in England and Wales working to improve law and practice for families with children in care.)

Grandparents Federation
Moot House, The Stow,
Harlow, Essex CM20 3AG
Tel: 01279 444964
(Support group for grandparents, particularly those whose grandchildren have gone into care.)

Lesbian and Gay Foster and Adoptive Parents Network (LAGFAPN)
c/o Stonewall
16 Clerkenwell Close, London EC1R 0AA
Tel: 0171 336 8860 Email: info@stonewall.org.uk

National Foster Care Association (NFCA)
87 Blackfriars Road,
London SE1 8HA
Tel: 0171 620 6400 Email: nfca@fostercare.org.uk
(Support and information for everyone involved in foster care.)

The National Organisation for Counselling Adoptees and their Parents (NORCAP)
112 Church Road
Wheatley, Oxfordshire OX33 1LU
Tel: 01865 875000
(Counselling and information service for adult adoptees searching for birth parents.)

Natural Parents Network (NPN)
c/o 3 Ashdown Drive, Mosley Common
Nr. Tyldesley, Manchester M28 1BR
(Support group for birth parents whose children have been placed for adoption.)
(National database for linking families with children needing adoption.)

Scottish Child's Law Centre
Cransdon House,
108 Argyle Street, Glasgow G2 8BH
Tel: 0141 226 3434

Stepfamily Association
Chapel House,
18 Hatton Place, London EC1N 8JN
Tel: 0171 209 2460
(Support and information for all stepfamilies.)

Stepfamily Scotland
5 Coates Place
Edinburgh EH3 7AA
Tel: 0131 225 8005

Independent services offering support and information to those involved in adoption from abroad

AFAA (Association of Families who have Adopted from Abroad)
c/o Buena Vista, Hawford Wood
Ombersley, Droitwich, Worcestershire WR9 0EZ
Tel: 01905 620005 Email: afaa@mati.demon.co.uk

OASIS (Overseas Adoption Support and Information Service)
Dan Y Craig, Balaclava Road
Glais, Swansea SA7 9HJ
Tel: 01792 844329 Email: oasis@ndirect.co.uk

Overseas Adoption Helpline
PO Box 13899
London N6 4WB
Tel: 0990 168742

Independent services offering after adoption support to anyone involved in adoption

Adoption Counselling Centre
Family Care
21 Castle Street, Edinburgh EH2 3DN
Tel: 0131 225 6441

After Adoption (Manchester and Surrounding Districts)
12–14 Chapel Street
Salford, Manchester M3 7NN
Tel: 0161 839 4930 Email: aadoption@aol.com

After Adoption Wales
Unit 1 Cowbridge Court
58–62 Cowbridge Road West, Cardiff CF5 5BS
Tel: 01222 575711 Email: aaw@dial.tipex.com

After Adoption Yorkshire
31 Moor Road
Headingly, Leeds LS6 4BG
Tel: 0113 230 2100

Merseyside Adoption Centre
316–317 Coopers Building
Church Street, Liverpool L1 3AA
Tel: 0151 709 9122

Post-Adoption Centre
5 Torriano Mews
Torriano Avenue, London NW5 2RZ
Tel: 0171 284 0555

Scottish Adoption Advice Centre
16 Sandyford Place
Glasgow G3 7NB
Tel: 0141 339 0772

Talkadoption
12–14 Chapel Street
Salford, Greater Manchester M3 7NN
Tel: 0800 783 1234

(A service for young people up to age 26 who are involved in adoption.)

West Midlands Post-Adoption Services (WMPAS)
92 Newcombe Road
Handsworth, Birmingham B21 8DD
Tel: 0121 523 3343